Fire HD6 Tips, Tricks, and Traps:

A How-To Tutorial for the Fire HD6

Edward Jones

Fire HD6 Tips, Tricks, and Traps by Edward Jones

Other Books by Edward Jones

Top 300 Free Apps for the Kindle Fire is your guide to 300 of the top rated apps that you'll find useful for your Fire. Jones has taken the time to research and compile this extensive list of apps for your Fire, and best of all, each of these apps are FREE. You'll find apps for the home office, for entertainment, for news, weather, and sports, for your health, for managing your finances, for playing games, and more. A local news apps section provides news, weather, and traffic apps for over 50 major US cities, and a travel section gives you an insight to the best apps that will help you find great deals on flights, hotel rooms, cruises, dining, and even the best gas prices around your hometown or when on the road. Each listing begins with a clickable link back to the Amazon catalog. So as you read this book on your Fire HD6, if any particular app sounds like what you've been looking for, just tap the image or heading name. You'll be taken directly to the Amazon page for the app, where you can click the button to install that app. (Active wi-fi connection required.) Let Top 300 Free Apps for the Kindle Fire be your guide to the best free apps for your new tablet!

Kindle Fire HDX Tips, Tricks, and Traps: A Tutorial for the Kindle Fire HDX. If you happen to own BOTH a Kindle Fire HDX, and a Kindle Fire HD6, you may already know that they are ***not*** the same device. In this comprehensive guide, you'll learn tips (ways to effectively use your Fire), tricks (ways to improve the operation of your Fire), and traps (things to avoid to prevent problems while using your Fire). Learn to use features that are new to the HDX line, including Google or Outlook Calendar and Contacts synchronization, Microsoft Exchange corporate e-mail support, and Amazon's 'Mayday' online technical support. This book also details how you can use the built-in cameras (front-facing in the 7-inch model, front-and-rear facing in the 8.9-inch model) to take photos and videos; how you can setup the security options to protect your account information; and how you can provide a safe environment for children using parental controls and Kindle FreeTime. If you own a Kindle Fire HDX, you owe it to yourself to get the book that's been written ***exclusively*** for the ***Kindle Fire HDX***! **(BOTH BOOKS are available through the Amazon Store and can be found with a search for 'kindle fire edward jones.')**

For a complete listing of my books, see my Author page on Amazon at-
amazon.com/author/edwardjones_writer

INTRODUCTION

So, you've got a Fire HD6 as a gift, or perhaps you bit the purchase bullet on your own because you wanted this awesome tablet. However you came into possession of your Fire HD6, you probably have unanswered questions about its operation, or would just love to get the most out of your new tablet. In this comprehensive guide, you'll learn tips (ways to effectively use your Fire HD6), tricks (ways to improve the operation of your Fire HD6), and traps (things to avoid to prevent problems while using your Fire HD6). You will learn-

- How to get around to the user interface, the home screen, and the carousel more efficiently
- How to make your Fire HD6 your own, customizing its display and operation for fastest and easiest use
- How to use the new household profiles feature to allow shared use of a Fire H6 by multiple users of the same household
- How to find THOUSANDS of FREE as in, 'zero dollars and zero cents') books
- How to use the built-in cameras to take photos and videos
- How to setup your e-mail accounts, including corporate accounts such as Microsoft Exchange
- How to setup the security options to protect your account information
- How you can move your iTunes or other music library to your Fire
- How you can download YouTube videos to your Fire
- Suggested apps that no Kindle Fire owner should be without

You will learn all of the above and more, with ***Fire HD6 Tips, Tricks, and Traps: A How-To Tutorial for the Fire HD6*** as a part of your library. Read on, and learn 100% of what you need to know to get the most out of your Fire HD6!

IMPORTANT NOTE: This book covers the Fire HD6, introduced by Amazon in September of 2014. If you are using any other model of Kindle Fire, please see our sister publications "Kindle Fire HD Tips, Tricks, and Traps," "Kindle Fire HD7 Tips, Tricks, and Traps," or "Kindle Fire HDX Tips, Tricks, and Traps."

Table of Contents

Chapter 1: Kindle Fire Out of the Box

Welcome to ***Fire HD6 Tips, Tricks, and Traps: A How-To Tutorial for the Fire HD6***. This is a user's guide, written to get beginners up to speed quickly, as well as to provide content that will also appeal to the more technically-savvy. In this book, you will find all the basic tips you need to quickly learn to use your Fire HD6 like a seasoned pro. And the more advanced topics covered in this book will help you take your use of the Fire HD6 to a higher level, getting the most out of your new tablet.

This book looks at three categories in every chapter: ***tips***, ***tricks***, **and** ***traps***.

Tips are techniques that make things easier in terms of use, in a particular area.

Tricks are techniques that change the operation of your Fire in a particular area, often providing capabilities or performance improvements that just were not there out of the box.

Traps are "gotchas," things to watch out for, that can cause problems.

About the Fire HD6

The Fire HD6 is one product in a line of products known as Amazon Kindles. Kindles are handheld devices, designed and sold by Amazon that let you shop for and view or download e-books, magazines, movies, TV shows, music, and other digital content using wireless technology. The Fire HD6 was released in September 2014, and is (at the time of this writing) unmatched in terms of outstanding features at a very affordable price. Sporting a 6-inch display and built-in speaker for audio playback, the Fire HD6 is quite an accomplishment for a device with prices starting at under $100 US at the time of this writing. The Fire HD6 is just one model within the Fire family, the others including the Fire HD7 with a 7-inch screen and stereo speakers, and the Fire HDX, in both 7-inch and 8.9-inch (diagonal measurement) screen sizes.

Amazon's Fire product line has been in existence for some time, with the first models introduced in 2011. Until September 2014, all products within the line were referred to under the name 'Kindle Fire.' With the September 2014 introduction of new models (including the Fire HD6), Amazon has dropped ‘Kindle’ from the names of the products, instead referring to all devices with color screens under the name ‘Fire’ (Fire HD6, Fire HD7, Fire HDX 7, and Fire HDX 8.9). Amazon now uses the name ‘Kindle’ exclusively for its e-ink (non-color) line of book readers, including the Kindle Touch, Kindle Paperwhite, and Kindle Voyager. This book refers to your device as the Fire HD6, but you are likely to see it referred to as a ‘Kindle Fire HD6’ at web sites and in other publications.

About tablet computers

The Fire HD6 falls price-wise at the low end and feature-wise in the midst of handheld computers generally referred to as tablets, and tablets occupy the market space between smartphones and laptop computers. Tablets generally possess all or nearly all the functions of laptop computers, two notable exceptions being that tablets generally lack physical keyboards and have smaller screens. The appealing feature of tablet computers is that they can run “apps.” Apps, short for applications, are small computer programs that run within the tablet’s internal memory and literally re-define the operation of the tablet. Apps can give your Fire HD6 the ability to act as far more than an e-book reader or a movie player. You can download and install apps that transform your Fire HD6 into a digital butler, an electronic medical advisor, a powerful financial analyst, or a first-rate handheld game platform.

About the ‘6’ in HD6

The number 6 is a reference to the diagonal measurement of screen size for the Fire HD6. While this may be a bit smaller than the very common 7-inch size of many Android tablets, the lower manufacturing costs make it possible for Amazon to provide such a feature-packed set for under $100. Within the tablet marketplace, the Fire HD6 compares favorably to other low-cost devices that typically sport 6 to 7-inch screens and run apps designed for the Android operating system. In the US market, there has been a flood of inexpensive Android tablets in the under $100 range, with wildly varying levels of quality and reliability. With the introduction of the Fire HD6, Amazon appears to be providing this market with a reliable and well-built device.

Where's My Data? (Your Fire HD6 Storage, and the Amazon Cloud)

With the popularity of tablets, you may have heard talk of what may be a somewhat magical and mystical place known as "the cloud." Your Fire HD6 has some built-in data storage of 8 gigabytes or 16 gigabytes, depending upon the memory option you chose when you purchased your HD6 (8 gigabytes being the standard amount).

This may sound like a lot of space, but in the grand scheme of things, it really is not. (By comparison, the average personal computer sold at the time of this writing typically has a 500 gigabyte or 1,000 gigabyte or “one terabyte” hard drive, and a single Blu-Ray DVD movie occupies roughly 25 gigabytes.) If you tried to store large amounts of digital content- especially movies and videos- on your Fire HD6, you would quickly exhaust its usable space. To get around this problem, all Amazon Fires (and many other tablets) store large amounts of information in the cloud, which is another name for data servers that are accessed from the Internet. Amazon's servers are referred to as the Amazon Cloud, and all Fire owners have access to unlimited amounts of data storage for their purchases in the Amazon cloud.

Content that you purchase from Amazon is stored in either of two places: in your cloud storage on Amazon's servers, and on your Fire itself. (Often, your content is stored in two places simultaneously: when you download an item, it is stored both on your device, and a copy of it remains in the Amazon cloud.) When you initially purchase a book, a song, a game, or an app (even free content is purchased, you just aren't charged for this), the content is initially stored in your personal space in the Amazon Cloud, where the content is not taking up any space on your Fire. When you press the Download button that appears on the icon for that content in the cloud, it gets downloaded to the memory space of your Fire itself.

If you display a given category on your Fire, such as apps, books, or music, at the top of the screen you will see icons for ***Cloud*** and ***Device***, as shown in the illustration that follows.

Tap Cloud to see all of the content that is stored on Amazon's cloud under your account, and tap Device to see all the content that you downloaded from the cloud onto your device. You can download content from the cloud onto your device anytime you have an active Wi-Fi connection, and you can delete content from the device as necessary to ensure that you have plenty of room for new content.

If you are curious as to whether you are running short of storage space on your device, you can quickly determine your available storage space remaining. Get to the Home screen, tap and drag down the Navigation bar at the top of the screen, and tap Settings at the upper right. Under Settings, tap Device Options at the next screen that appears, then tap Storage. Your Kindle Fire will display a Storage screen, similar to the example shown in the following illustration.

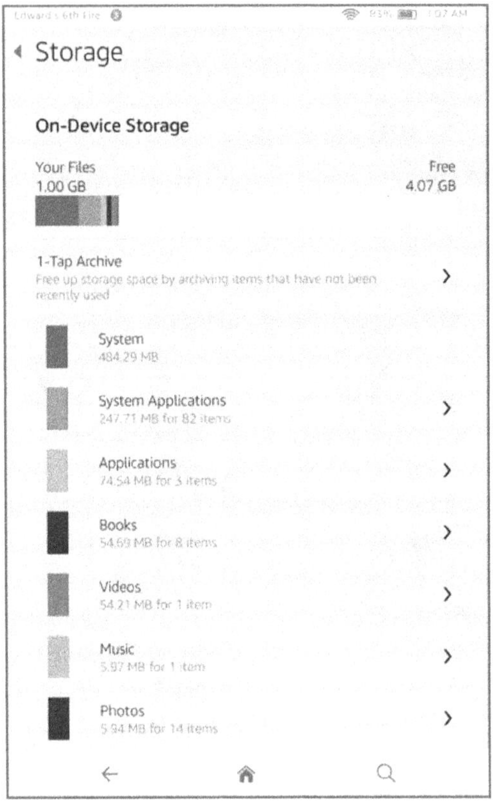

The Storage screen tells you how much space is available, and how much space is currently being used by various categories, such as books and newsstand items, audio books, music, videos, and photos.

History of the Fire HD6

This portion of this chapter certainly isn't required reading if you are to become an accomplished user of your Fire HD6, but it is a fascinating success story. The Fire HD6 is one of a line of products that all sprang from the original Amazon Kindle, a revolutionary device inspired by a revolutionary individual, Amazon founder and CEO Jeff Bezos. During the nascent days of the World Wide Web, it was Bezos who came up with the idea of selling books online, rather than in the traditional bricks and mortar bookstore environment, and Bezos founded Amazon, billed as the world's largest bookstore. Books were very good to Bezos and to Amazon, catapulting the company to a multibillion dollar global enterprise and taking Bezos to billionaire status in the process. But even though Bezos himself was (and is, according to reports) an avid book reader, he recognized something: a cornerstone of Amazon's long-term future in the 21st century, the printed book, was a likely candidate for obsolescence by the end of the 21st century, if not sooner. Music had gone digital, video was in the process of moving in that direction, and for the printed book, the same transition was simply a matter of time. Having built a better bookstore, Bezos believed he could improve upon one of humanity's greatest inventions- the printed book- by taking it digital.

In 2004, Bezos turned a group of engineers loose in an Amazon subsidiary, Lab126, based in Cupertino, California, and charged them with the task of developing a digital replacement for the printed book. Roughly three years later, in November of 2007, Amazon placed the fruits of Bezos dream and the engineers' labors- the original Amazon Kindle- on sale. It used a patented E-ink display that was capable of rendering 16 shades to simulate reading on paper while using minimal amounts of power. Content for the Amazon Kindle could be purchased online and downloaded wirelessly. (The name "Kindle" was the brainchild of consultants hired by the Lab126 division of Amazon, who felt that like kindling, it had the potential to light a fire- and that is exactly what the device began to do in the book publishing world.)

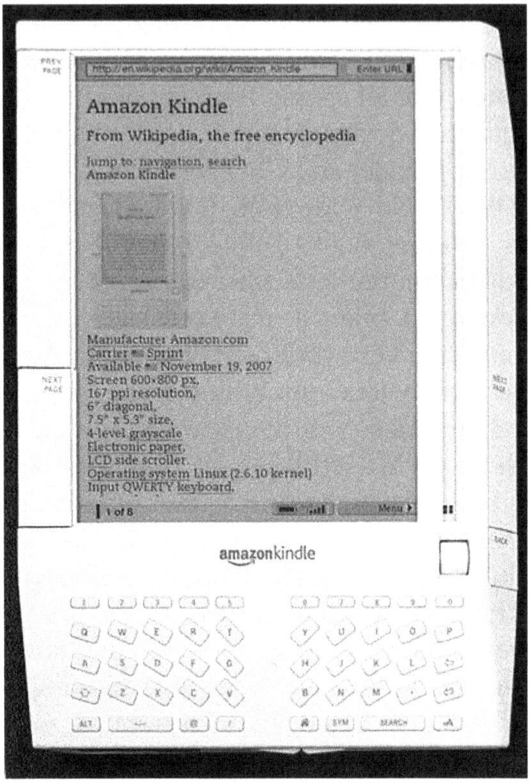

First Amazon Kindle (photo credit: Wikipedia)

Despite the fact that the device cost nearly $400 US, Amazon sold out its initial manufacturing run in a little over five and one half hours, and the Kindle remained out of stock until late April of 2008. The success of the original Amazon Kindle led to a family of devices, and as technology continued to advance and manufacturing costs continued to drop, the original Kindle Fire became a product in Amazon's Kindle family. Announced in September of 2011, the original Kindle Fire was Amazon's first Kindle to sport a liquid crystal display-based color screen, rather than the patented black on white E-ink display used by all the earlier Kindles. The original Fire not only included access to Amazon's AppStore, but could also display streaming movies and TV shows as well as run 'apps,' in addition to being used to read books.

To say that the product has been successful would be an understatement: by May, 2013, the Amazon Fire product line was the second best-selling tablet after Apple's iPad, with about seven million units sold, according to research estimates (source: Wikipedia). And while there's still a number of years left to this 21st century, the handwriting is clearly on the wall with regards to the eventual demise of the paper-based book. The Association of American Publishers reported that in the first quarter of 2012, e-book sales surpassed those of their paper-based counterparts for the first time- adult eBook sales were reported at $282.3 million, while adult hardcover sales during that same period reached only $229.6 million.

Setting up your Fire HD6

Set up your Fire now if it is fresh out of the box. If you've just opened up your Fire HD6's box, you'll need to turn it on and set it up before you can start using it.

If your Fire is fresh out of the box, you'll need to power up your new tablet and you'll need to set it up before you can begin using it. Before you start, make sure you have your Amazon username and password, and you will also need to be within range of an active Wi-Fi connection.

When you first turn your Fire on, you'll be asked to choose your language. After doing this, you'll select a Wi-Fi network and enter a password (if yours is a secured network).

The next screen that appears will ask you for registration information. You'll now need to register your Fire HD6. Enter your Amazon account details, or, if you don't have an Amazon account, choose create an account and follow the instructions that appear on the screen.

Next, you'll get to choose your time zone, and confirm your account information. Make your selections and tap Continue, and you will be asked if you wish t enable automatic backup to the Amazon cloud. Thus is recommended by Amazon, as the automatic backup feature keeps any files that you create on your Fire, such as pictures and videos you shoot, as well as music that you may add to your device.

After choosing whether to enable automatic backup, you will be given the option to set up your Facebook and/or Twitter accounts. (You can do this now, or skip this step and save this for later.)

Finally, you will see some on-screen hints and tips that will help you get started with your Fire HD6. If you already have Kindle content linked to your device, or apps from the Amazon App Store, they will all be available for download from the Amazon Cloud (more on this topic shortly). Your recently-read Kindle books will appear in an area known as the carousel automatically, along with the latest apps and other downloaded content.

Controls and Layout of the Fire HD6

Take the time to get familiar with the physical aspects of your Fire. Looking at the front\ of the device, with the volume rocker switch at the upper right, the following illustration shows the layout of various components.

Fire HD6, front view (artwork courtesy Amazon, Inc.)

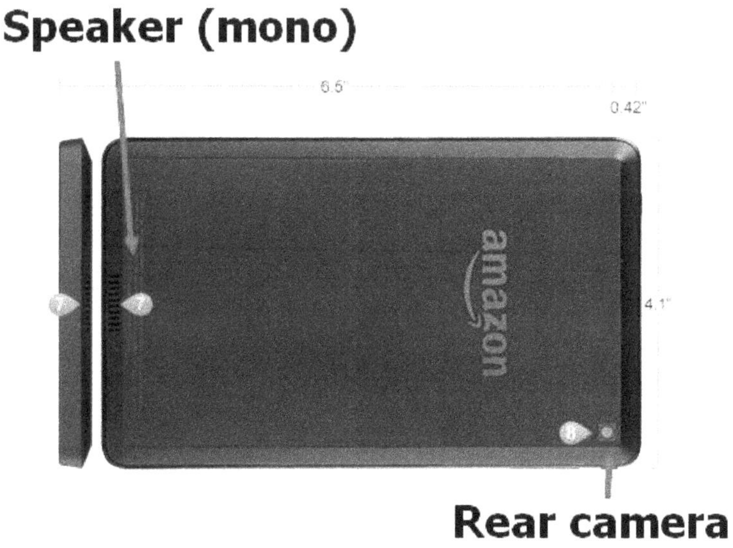

Fire HD6, rear view (artwork courtesy Amazon, Inc.)

Get familiar with the various parts of the Fire's user interface. The next chapter will detail this area extensively, but out of the box, it helps to know about the areas that you will be working with on your Fire HD6 screen. The following illustration shows these areas.

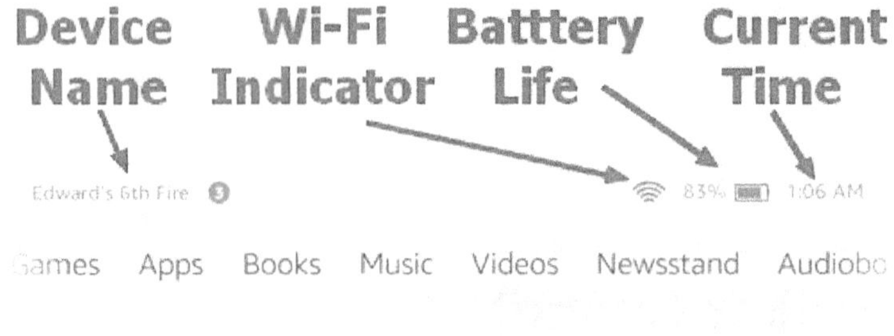

(upper part of Fire's screen)

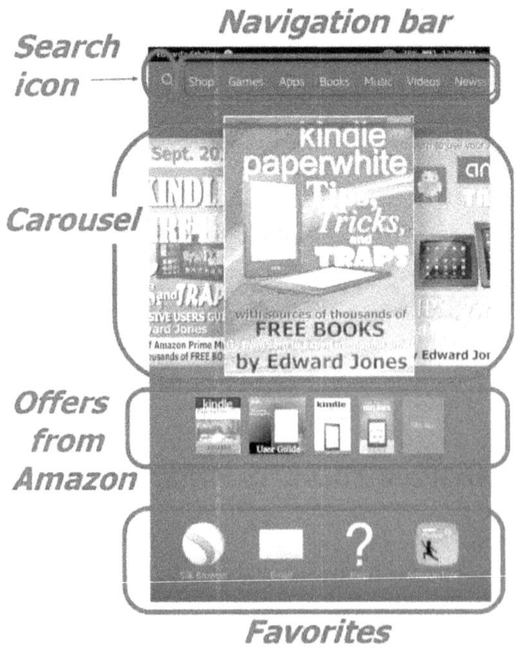

(Fire HD6 display)

You can get quick access to items that you use regularly by placing them in your Favorites area. (You can view all of your favorites by swiping the entire screen upwards with one finger on the Fire HD6.) To add a book, periodical, or app to your favorites area, first use the Navigation bar at the top of the screen. When the desired category appears, press and hold a desired item until a highlighted menu bar appears at the top of the screen, then tap the Home icon in this area.

To install any saved apps, in the Navigation Bar tap on Apps, then tap on the Cloud tab. Tap on any of the icons to start that particular app downloading onto your device.

You can import your iTunes or similar music collection from your computer to your Fire. To import an existing music collection, you'll have to set up the Amazon Cloud Player on your tablet. Open a browser window on your computer, and visit amazon.com/cloudplayer (if you are in North America) or visit amazon.co.uk/cloudplayer (if you are in the United Kingdom) to begin importing the music from your computer into Cloud Player, which can then be streamed or downloaded onto your Fire HD6.

Having problems??? When in doubt, reboot. Your Fire HD6 is a sophisticated computer, and like all computers, it may hiccup for unexplainable reasons at times. If your Fire HD freezes or locks up and refuses to respond to any actions, perform a hard reset. (You needn't worry about losing any memory settings with this type of reset; it just halts any programs currently running and shuts down your device.) Hold the power button depressed until you see a 'Shutdown your Fire?' message appear on the screen, and then tap Yes.' Wait another 10 seconds, then turn on your Fire.

If you are experiencing an unusually high number of system lock-ups, make sure your battery charge level is not very low. A nearly fully-drained battery is a common cause of random Fire freezes.

Chapter 2: User-Interface Tips, Tricks, and Traps

The ***user interface*** (that's techno-speak for "the way you get along with the device") is fairly intuitive on any Amazon Fire, and that is by design. Amazon engineers have done a credible job of making the tablet easy to use, and with a market dominated by a product like Apple's iPad, that was an understandable goal. Nevertheless, there are things that you can do to make the way that you use your Fire more efficient, and that is what this chapter is all about.

About the Home Screen, Navigation Bar, Carousel, and Favorites

The Fire HD6 is based on a heavily modified version of Google's Android operating system. For the technically minded among readers, the Fire HD6 and other current models in the Fire line (including both Fire HDX models) use the "KitKat" version of the Android operating system that Google developed exclusively for Amazon, known as Fire 4.0 O/S.

In any case, all Fires make use of a user interface that is very different than that of a generic Android tablet. Power up a Fire and you won't see the desktop like design of an Android tablet. Instead, you will see Amazon's own customized interface called the Home screen, shown in the next illustration. Pardon the intentional repetition, but the illustration, which was shown in the prior chapter, is displayed once more here. In this chapter, we go into more detail about the parts of the Fire user interface, and how you can best use these features.

(The Home screen of the Fire HD6)

From the Home screen, your books, apps, music, and videos are all accessible with a swipe of the ***Navigation Bar***. Simply swipe the Navigation bar to the left or right and tap the desired category such as apps, games, books, music, or videos to display all of the items within that category. At the far left of the Navigation bar there is a ***Search icon*** (in the shape of a magnifying glass) that can be used to search the entire device content, to search Amazon's massive library of content, or to just search the web.

Displaying your Favorites

Whenever the Home screen is visible, you can view all of your favorites by simply swiping upwards on the entire screen. When you do this, your favorites will come into view, similar to the example shown in the following illustration. Tap any favorite to open that item.

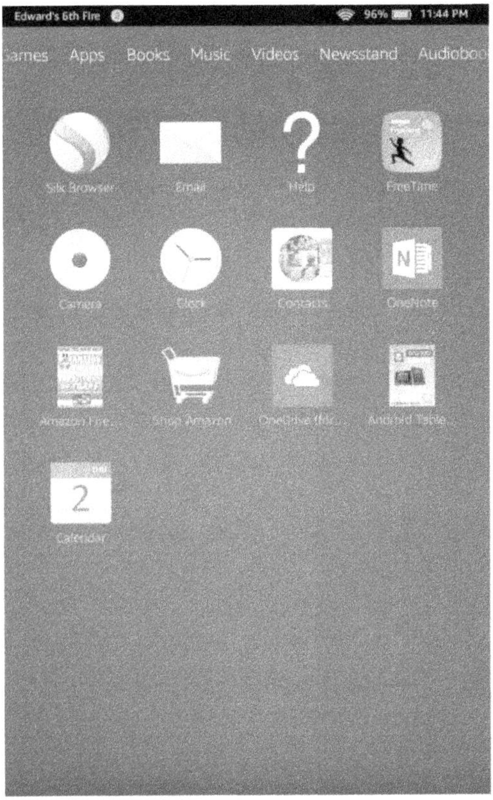

The center area of the Home screen displays the ***Carousel***. The Carousel will contain an assortment of icons for all of the items that you've recently accessed on your Fire, whether they are books, songs, magazines, movies, or web pages.

Understand the difference between the *Carousel* and your *Favorites*. The Carousel grows dynamically as you use your Fire, because an icon for everything that you've recently used on your Fire will appear on the Carousel and will remain for some time unless you delete it from the Carousel. With your Favorites, on the other hand, nothing appears automatically. You must add an item to the Favorites area in order for it to appear. (On a new Fire, it's true that a few items appear in the Favorites area, but Amazon added these items so that the Favorites would not be empty. Clearly, these are not your favorites, so you'll probably want to get rid of them.)

You can get quick access to items that you use regularly by placing them in your Favorites. You can view all of your favorites by swiping the entire screen upwards with one finger. To add a book, song, movie, game, or app to your favorites area, first use the Navigation bar at the top of the screen. When the desired category appears, press and hold a desired item until a menu of icons appears at the top of the screen, then tap the Home icon in this area.

Clean up your Carousel. Over time, your Carousel can become overly cluttered with icons for all the items you've accessed on your Fire. To delete items from the carousel, press and hold the unwanted item until a menu of icons appears at the top of the screen, then tap the Remove icon in this area.

Know how to come home. One of the first things any young child learns is how to come home, and any new Fire user should know how to get to the home screen as well. From anywhere you are at, tap in the center of the screen, and the home icon will appear at the lower center, as shown in the following illustration. Tap Home and you will return to the home screen.

Setting your Display

Adjust your font sizes to make reading easiest on YOU. The Fire HD6 is a great multimedia device, but the entire Kindle line began life as an e-book reader, and millions of people still use it primarily for that purpose. You can easily adjust the font sizes to fit your needs. With any book open, tap in the center of the screen, and then tap the View (Aa) icon at the top of the screen. You will see a dialog box like the one shown in the following illustration:

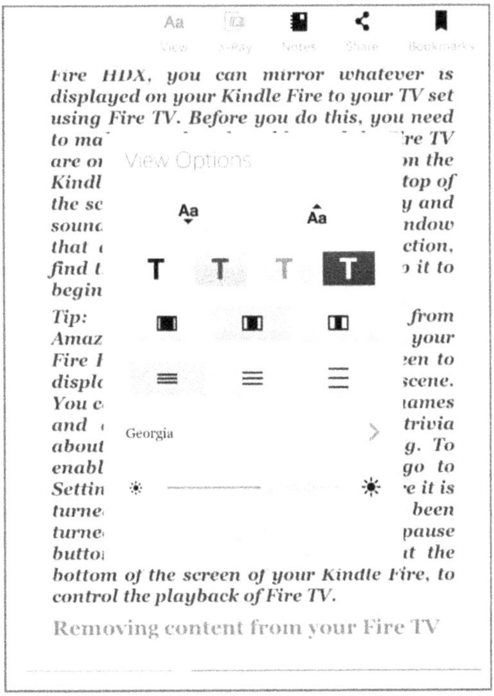

Tap the small letters 'Aa' to shrink the text, or tap the large letters 'Aa' to enlarge the text. You can also try the different Color Mode settings (white, soft green, sepia, and black) to see if you prefer one of these different backgrounds for your book reading. The lower rows within the dialog box contain buttons that let you adjust the margin width or the line spacing. And you can tap the Font name list box (displaying 'Georgia' in this illustration) to display additional fonts that you can choose for your display.

Tap the 'More Settings' link at the bottom of the dialog box, and another screen appears where you can choose to turn on Popular Highlights and Text-to-Speech options. These options, enabled by the publishers of some books and periodicals, allow for the display of highlighted items that other readers find to be popular, and allow for the reading of text aloud, using the built-in speaker or the headphone jack of your Fire.

Note that the Kindle display settings will control the text display of most e-books, but may not have an effect on some magazines. Many of the magazine publishers use their own settings menus to change the way the magazine is displayed.

Customizing your Favorites

Edit and rearrange your Favorites. Any items that you recently accessed will appear on the Carousel. You can add any of these items to your Favorites so that you can gain fast access to regularly used items by swiping the entire screen upwards. Just find the item in your Carousel, press and hold until a large check mark appears in the center of the items image, and then press the 'Home' icon that appears at the top of the screen.

You can rearrange the items in your Favorites area to suit your liking. Just long-press on an item until it dims in brightness, then slide your finger to a new location. The remaining favorites will automatically rearrange themselves.

Use 'Search' to find anything stored on your Kindle. While many Fire users think of the search field as a way to search for content such as books or movies, you can actually use the Search field to find any item that is stored on your device. Just go to the Home screen, tap the magnifying glass to bring up the Search field, and type a few letters. Search will bring up all items- books, videos, music, games, and so on- that match the letters you've typed. Tap anywhere above the keyboard to put the keyboard away, scroll to the desired item, and tap the item to open the item or launch an app.

Adding household profiles

A major addition to the newest Fire products is the ability to create household profiles, letting you share a single Fire HD6 among multiple members of your household. (The improvement is actually a part of the new Fire 4.0 operating system, so if you own any 4th-generation Fire such as the HD-6 or HD-7, or any 3rd-generation Fire that has received the Fire 4.0 OS update, you can make use of this feature.) You can add one adult and up to four children as members with their own profiles. With household profiles implemented, the carousel, favorites, and content that each household member sees are unique to that individual.

 ***If you are adding an adult, that person will need to log in with their own Amazon account credentials to complete the process. Make sure that persons' account information is available before continuing with these steps. (Child profiles will not need their own Amazon accounts.)***

Creating an adult profile

To create a household profile for an adult, swipe down from the top of the screen and tap Settings, then tap Personal Profiles, and then tap Add Adult. At this point, you will see the 'Add Adult Profile' screen, as shown in the following illustration.

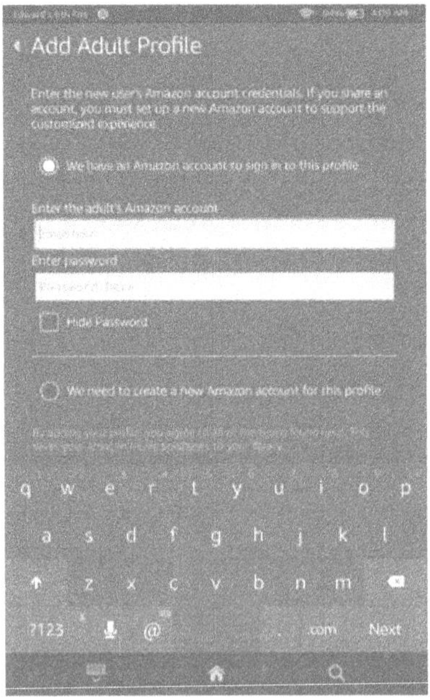

The adult must now log in using their Amazon account credentials, or create a new account if they do not have their own Amazon account. Fill in the information needed for the adult profile, and tap Next. You can then proceed to add child profiles if desired, using the following steps.

Creating a child profile

To create a household profile for a child, swipe down from the top of the screen and tap Settings, then tap Personal Profiles, and then tap Add Child. At this point, you will see the 'Add Child Profile' screen, as shown in the following illustration.

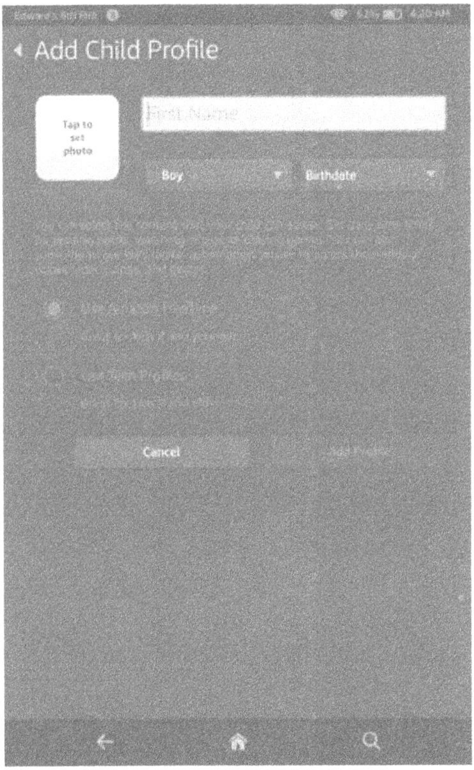

You will be asked to enter the child's name, birthday, and gender. You can also tap the picture icon at the upper left to choose a pre-selected image to identify the child at the login screen, or you can tap 'User photo' to select a personal photo from the gallery. You will also need to select whether the content within the child's profile should be limited by Kindle FreeTime, or whether the profile should be a less-restrictive teen profile. Fill in the requested information, and tap 'Create profile' to add the child profile to your Fire HD6. (For additional details about Kindle FreeTime and how you can use this feature to shield young ones from inappropriate content, see Chapter 11.)

Once a child profile has been created, an additional screen will appear (see the following example), and you must approve the content that will be made available to the child.

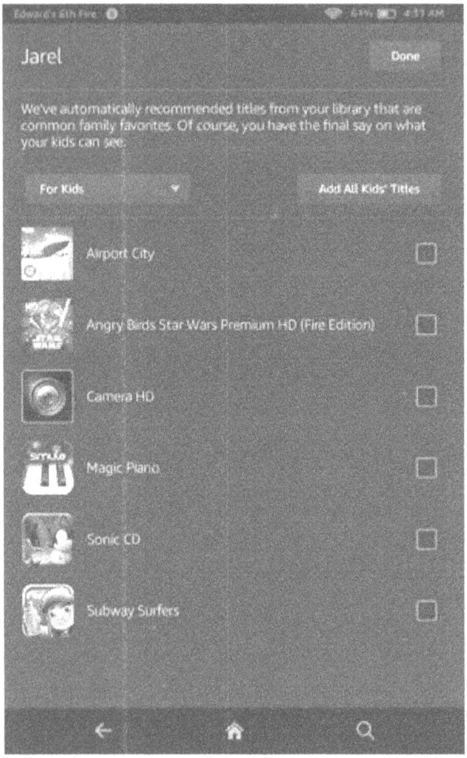

Tap the drop-down menu at the upper-left and choose from 'Books', 'Videos', 'Apps', or 'All' to display your content, then check the boxes beside the content that you want made available to the child. When finished, click the 'Done' button at the upper-right.

Switching profiles

You can switch between profiles by simply turning your Fire tablet off and back on. Press the power button twice, to turn the tablet off and back on. Tap the profile icon that now appears in the upper-left corner of the screen (as shown in the following illustration), then tap the icon for the profile that you wish to use. (If you are switching to an adult profile, you will be prompted for the lock code for that profile.)

Editing or removing household profiles

Once household profiles exist, you can edit or delete a given profile. To do so, swipe down from the top of the screen and tap Settings, then tap Household Profiles to display the household profiles screen, shown here.

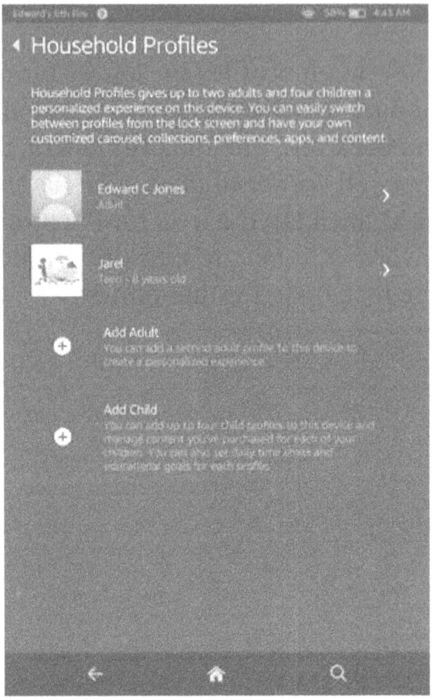

Tap the profile that you want to change, and make the desired changes. (When a profile is visible, you can tap 'Remove from household' to remove the profile, likely the appropriate action to take once your "child" has departed for college!)

If you remove an adult profile from a household, that adult's Amazon account cannot be added to another set of household profiles for 180 days.

Household profiles make shared use of a Fire tablet a simple matter. One point that you'll want to keep in mind regarding child profiles is that as your children grow older and as you purchase new content, you'll likely want to update their profiles accordingly.

Changing Basic Settings on your Fire

Know your status. At the top of your Fire, just above the Navigation bar, is an area known as the Status bar. Here, you will see any notifications indicated by a number inside a small circle, a wi-fi signal strength indicator, and the battery life indicator. Tap and drag down anywhere within the Status bar area to reveal various settings for your Fire, as shown in the following illustration:

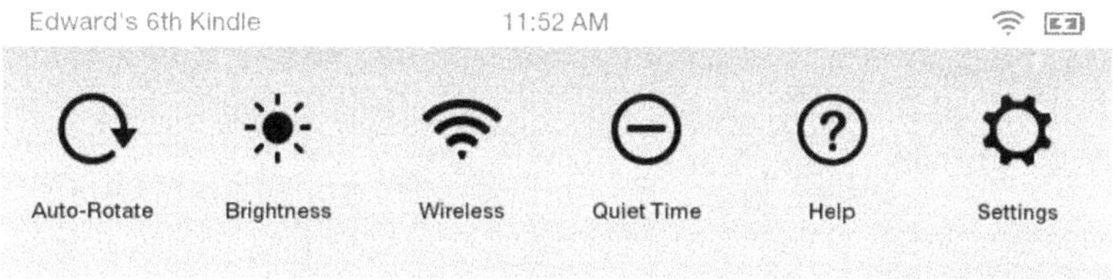

Auto-rotate: your Fire contains a gyroscope, which senses when the device is rotated, causing the display to shift between portrait and landscape mode. There are times when this is more of an annoyance than a help, such as when you are reading with the Fire lying on a flat surface such as a tabletop. Tap the Auto-rotate icon to change the setting to 'rotation-locked,' to disable the auto rotate function.

Brightness: tap the brightness icon to reveal a slider bar that you can slide up or down to increase or decrease screen brightness.

Wireless: Tapping the wireless option brings up another screen which lets you enable or disable Airplane Mode (turning off wireless transmission for when you are using your Fire in flight), along with an option to enable Bluetooth device settings (for sharing data with other Bluetooth-equipped devices such as many modern laptops, portable keyboards, and some smart phones). There's a VPN option, which can be used to securely connect to virtual private networks used by many businesses.

You will also find an option to allow or prevent Location Based Services from estimating your location. Also present on this screen is a Wi-Fi option that, when tapped, displays all wireless networks that are broadcasting in your area, similar to the example shown in the following illustration.

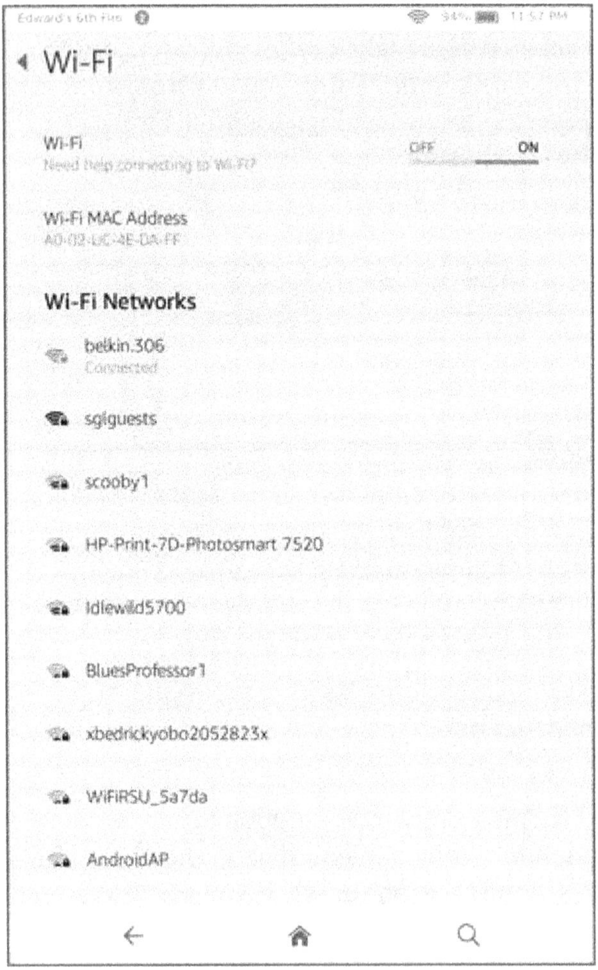

On this screen, select the desired Wi-Fi network by name. If the network is protected, you will be asked for the security key, and you must enter the security key before your Fire will connect to your Wi-Fi network.

If you don't remember what the security key is for your own home Wi-Fi network, look on the bottom of the cable modem or the phone company router that provides your Wi-Fi service. Many Wi-Fi routers provided by cable and telephone companies have the password written on a sticker on the underside of the modem.

Quiet Time: This option lets you turn on "quiet time," disabling any popup notifications and muting all sounds for message notifications such as e-mail or calendar alerts.

Help: This icon, when pressed, displays a help screen that lets you get help with wireless connectivity issues, open the user guide for your Fire HD6, or contact Amazon customer service, either via e-mail or by phone.

Settings: Tapping the settings icon will display a settings screen, as shown in the example that follows.

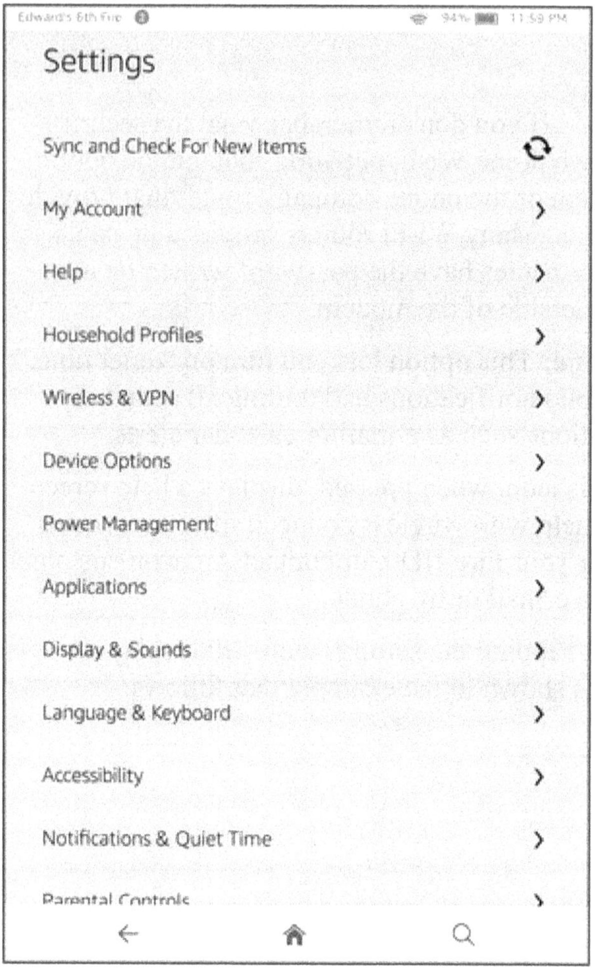

From here, you can access a variety of settings for your Fire HD6, by simply tapping on the appropriate subcategory within the Settings screen. For example, you can tap the Display and Sounds subcategory to display a screen that lets you adjust the volume and or the screen brightness, and you can tap the Security subcategory to create a locking password that prevents your Fire from being used by unauthorized users who do not know the password that you set for your device. You'll find many of these individual subcategories and their options explained in further detail in later parts of this book.

Of particular interest is the Device Options subcategory under the Settings screen. (To get here, drag down the Notifications bar at the top of the screen, and tap the Settings icon at the upper-right. In the Settings screen, tap Device Options to reveal the screen shown in the following illustration.) Here you can gain access to a number of settings that govern the individual behavior of your Fire HD6.

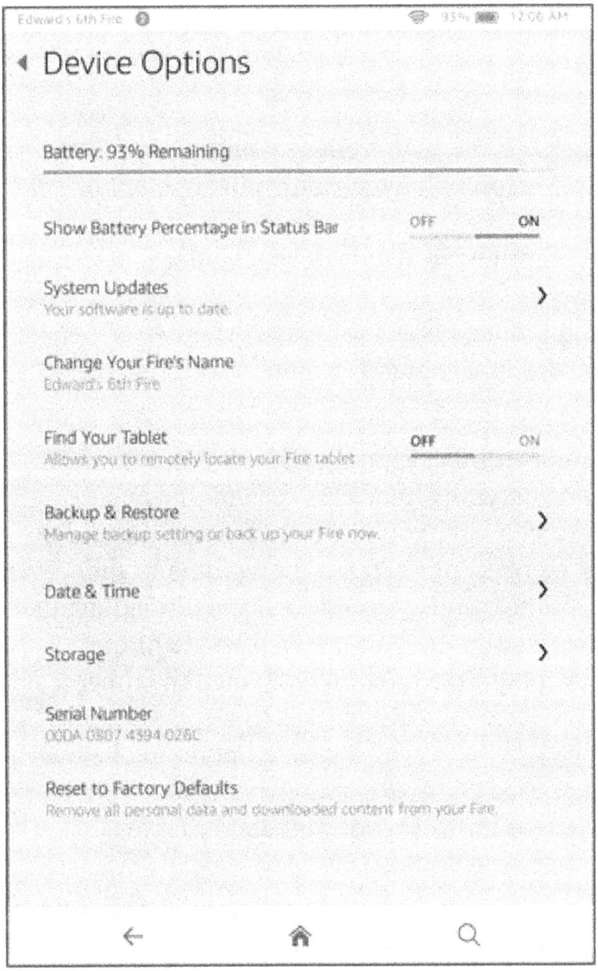

The Device Options screen provides a visual indication of the state of your battery charge, options for changing your tablet's name and finding your tablet remotely, and the storage space utilized by various applications such as books, magazines, movies, music, and so forth. You can perform backup and restore operations from the Amazon cloud, adjust your date and time settings, and even reset the device to its original factory settings (useful when it is time to upgrade to a more powerful Fire HDX, and pass on your trusted Fire HD6 to a close friend or relative).

If you return to the settings screen, you will see a number of options for controlling the overall behavior of your Fire. A few of the more popular options on this screen are described below:

Sync and check for new items: -tapping 'Sync and check for new items' icon will synchronize the content of your Fire with the Amazon Cloud, and your email, contacts, and calendar will be synchronized with external sources, assuming you have set up these external sources. Also, note that you can find out how to setup the external sources such as your e-mail, contacts, and calendar in Chapter 7, Email Tips, Tricks and Traps.)

Display and Sounds: -tapping 'Display and Sounds' displays another screen with slider bars for volume and display brightness on the screen, and you can finger swipe the slider bar left or right to increase or decrease the volume or the screen brightness (although it's admittedly easier to adjust the volume simply by pressing the buttons on the side of the device.) Use the Display Sleep option to change the time length, in minutes, before the device goes to sleep during periods of inactivity, and use the Font Size option to change the default font size used for text displayed outside of books and magazines (such as in the menus and dialog boxes presented by the operating system).

Language and keyboard: -tapping 'Language and keyboard' causes another screen to appear, containing options that let you set the language used for display of menu items and of the text displayed on all system screens. You will also find options for changing various keyboard settings, and options for pairing a wireless Bluetooth keyboard.

General Typing and Text-Entry Tips

Make the keyboard larger. Most Fire apps work in portrait or landscape mode, and the keyboard is much larger and easier to use in landscape mode. Rotate the Fire 90 degrees to get a landscape view of the keyboard, for an easier typing experience.

When typing large amounts of text, end each sentence with a fast double-space. Heavy duty word processing on a Fire (or any similarly sized tablet) is going to be somewhat challenging due to the combination of a soft keyboard and small screen size. One time saving tip when doing a lot of typing on the Fire is at the end of each sentence, tap the spacebar quickly twice. A fast double-space will automatically insert a period, followed by a single space. You can then continue on to the next sentence.

Use the 'predictive keyboard' feature to quickly type entire words. As you are typing text, you will notice a series of words appears just above the top row of the keyboard. These are words representing your Fire's best guess as to what you are typing, as shown in the following illustration:

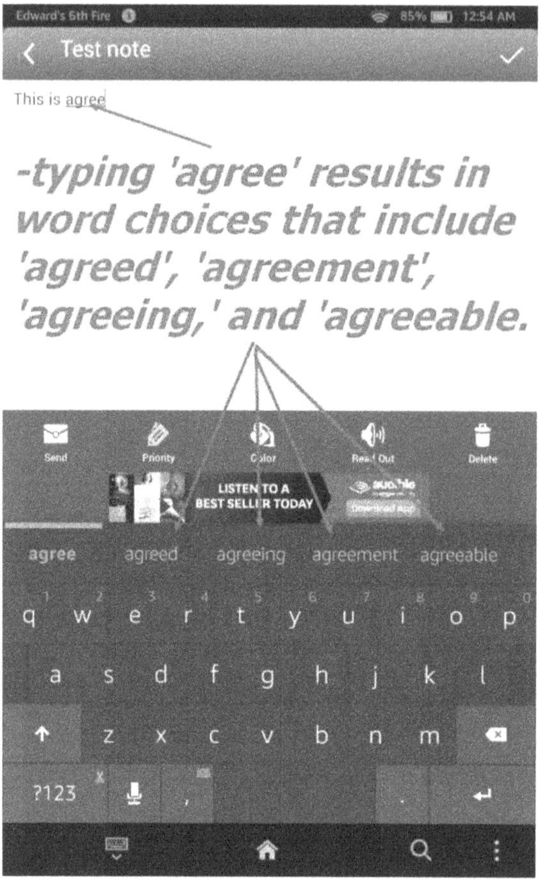

At any point, you can tap one of the word choices to add that word to your sentence.

The Fire really does have a Caps Lock key. For those times when you need to type a string of characters as ALL UPPERCASE LETTERS, the Fire does have the equivalent of a PC's Caps Lock key. Just double-tap the Shift key, and a square block will appear around the Shift symbol on the key indicator indicating that you are in Caps Lock mode. Type your upper case letters, then press the Shift key once more to drop out of Caps Lock mode.

Use the numbers shortcut to quickly enter numbers. If you are typing text, you don't need to switch between the letters keyboard and the numbers and symbols keyboard just to enter a number. The top row of letters can be long-pressed to enter a number. From left to right, a long-press on any of the top row of keys produce numbers from 1 through 9, followed by 0. Press and hold a top row letter until a number appears above the depressed key, then release, to type that number.

Your finger can serve as an insertion pointer. When editing large amounts of text, tap your finger on any empty area to display the Editing Tool. You can then press on it and move your fingertip within the text that you already typed, then release and edit the text as desired. When done editing, tap again at the end of the text, and continue typing.

Access the Cut-Copy-and-Paste options with a long-press on any word. If you need to cut or copy and paste during text editing, long-press on any single word, and cut / copy / paste editing options will appear, along with two selection handles. Drag the selection handles to highlight the desired text, then long-press on the desired text, and choose Cut or Copy. To paste the cut or copied text elsewhere, just long press at the desired location, and tap Paste.

Chapter 3: Let's go shopping!

Amazon has integrated the Fire HD6 to provide a first class shopping experience through the Amazon stores. (The phrase 'stores', plural, is intentional, because with the company's growth, Amazon has divided their online retail store into a collection of stores.) You can think of it as having all of the convenience of a mall-- different stores, each specializing in carrying a broad assortment of products in a specific area-- with none of the disadvantages of a mall (noisy crowds, unruly teenagers, or bad food at the food court). At the time of this writing, Amazon has divided its digital stores into eight categories: books, music, videos, newsstand, apps, games, audiobooks, and Amazon Prime. At the Home screen, tap Shop, and you will see links for the different stores at the left side of the page that appears, as shown in the illustration which appears on the following page.

To make shopping easier, you will probably want to set up 1-Click ordering as a payment method. 1-Click ordering places your order automatically, letting you skip the hassle of a digital shopping cart. When you place your first order at Amazon and enter a payment method and shipping address, 1-Click ordering is enabled automatically. If you click Buy now with 1-Click on any product page, your order is automatically charged to the default payment method registered to your account, and it is shipped to the default address.

You can also use 1-click to ship to multiple shipping addresses. Perhaps you wish to have some items shipped to you at your job, others at your primary home, and some at your vacation home. Login to your Amazon account through a web browser, and click Manage Your Account. At the next screen, click Manage Addresses and 1-Click Settings. At the next screen that appears, you can enter more than one shipping address.

When you save multiple shipping addresses, and you order an item, a list box with all of your addresses will appear. You can then choose the desired address to have the item shipped to that location.

Note: You must have cookies enabled within your computers' web browser to use 1-Click shopping. ("Cookies" are small chunks of data stored by your browser which are used by Amazon, as well as by many online banks and stores, to identify your account.) If you have not enabled cookies within your browser, you can still purchase items by adding them to the Amazon Shopping Cart, and clicking Proceed to checkout when you are ready to complete your order.

Buying books, magazines, and periodicals

Once you've connected wirelessly and you've set up your 1-click payment option at Amazon, you can easily purchase books, magazines, and newspapers from Amazon, and automatically download your purchases to your Fire. Tap at the top of the screen and tap the Home icon to get to your Home screen, then in the Navigation bar tap Shop, and the Amazon Kindle Store will appear on your screen, as shown in the illustration earlier in this chapter. You can browse among the various categories or search for items using the Search box at the upper right. Once you've located a desired item, you can tap Buy to download the book or periodical, or you can tap Try a Sample to download the start of the book for free.

Once you purchase an item, it is stored in your own library in the Amazon Cloud, and you can download it to your Fire HD6 as well as any other Kindles that you may own. You can also read your purchases using any of the free Kindle Reader Apps available for most personal computers and smartphones.

Buying or renting movies or TV shows

The hassle-free way to purchase or rent movies or TV shows and watch them on your Fire HD6 is to do so using Amazon's Video store, since it is so tightly integrated with the device. You can rent videos, in which case you get to watch the video for a specified time period. (The clock doesn't begin ticking until you first begin watching the video.) Alternately, you can purchase a video, in which case you can watch it whenever you like. There are just three simple steps involved in choosing and watching a video from Amazon's Video Store on your Fire HD6:

1. At the Home screen, tap Videos.

2. In the Search box, enter your video's title, **OR** swipe out from the screen's left edge to browse the Video store.

3. When you find the video you want, tap **Rent** or **Buy**.

For most videos, you will see an option to purchase either standard definition or high definition. The cost of the rental or purchase gets charged to your 1-click billing account at Amazon.

Your video experience will be unacceptable without a high-speed internet connection. Viewing movies or TV shows on your Fire HD6 (or on any tablet computer) requires the availability of a high-speed internet connection. If your internet speed is slow, you will see noticeable lags in your video playback. Your home network should be providing at least 2 MB of download speed for standard definition, and 4 MB of download speed for high-definition video. If you are sufficiently fortunate to own one of the newer ultra-high definition TV sets, you are looking at a minimum of 15 MB of continuous download speed for streaming. (You can test your network's speed by going to a free speed testing site, such as www.speedtest.net.) Also, be aware that ***each device*** on a home network adds to the streaming workload. You may think that your ten-megabit high-speed connection from your local cable company should suffice. However, if two parents have an iPad and a Fire HDX, four kids have their own Fire H6 tablets, two of the neighbors' kids who are visiting have their own tablets and all eight devices are streaming from the same network at the same time, the network is badly overloaded.

Serious videophile? Consider Amazon Prime and / or Netflix. If you are a major fan of watching movies and television shows, the author has two recommendations for you. The first is that you seriously consider becoming a member of Amazon Prime. For an annual fee of under $100 (at the time of this writing), in addition to the free two day shipping on a variety of items, you will also get to watch thousands of movies and shows from the Amazon Prime video library at no cost. Prime members can also stream movies and TV shows. The second recommendation is that you seriously consider a subscription to Netflix. You can then download the Netflix app at no cost from the Amazon AppStore, log into your Netflix account, and enjoy any one of the thousands of movies and shows available on Netflix.

Buying and downloading music from Amazon's MP3 Store

You can browse, shop for, and purchase your favorite music hits and download music from Amazon's MP3 Store using your Fire HD6; the following three steps are all that's necessary. (If you're outside the United States, see the note at the end of this section.)

1. At the Home screen, tap Music, and then tap Store.

2. In the Search box, enter your song or album title, **OR** swipe out from the screen's left edge to browse the Music store.

Narrow your search to quickly find what you are looking for. You can narrow your search by swiping out from the left side of the screen and then tapping Bestsellers, New Releases, or Browse Genres.

3. When you locate the desired song or album, tap the button that displays the price, then confirm your purchase by tapping the Buy button. (In some cases, the songs are free, and if that is the case you will see a Get button. You can tap this button to get the song.)

Try before you buy. If you want to listen to a sample of a song before purchasing the song, tap the 'Play' link (a triangle within a circle) beside the song's title. You'll hear a 30 second sample of the song.

Once you purchase a song or music album, it is in your account in the Amazon Cloud. You can download a song to your Fire HD6 at any time, by going to your Home page, tapping Music, tapping Cloud, and locating the desired song or album. Do a long-press (press and hold) on the song title or album cover until a popup menu appears, then choose 'Download' from the popup menu to download the song to your device.

NOTE: Copyright laws regarding music very from nation to nation. In order to buy music from Amazon's US-based MP3 store, you must have an Amazon account, a United States billing address, and a 1-click payment method that's been issued by a U.S. bank. And if you're using an Amazon gift card to make purchases, you must be physically located in the United States to use the Amazon MP3 Store. Amazon customers located within the United Kingdom can access the UK based MP3 store by going to www.amazon.co.uk and clicking the Music link.

Removing content from your device

Remove reading content and downloaded movies you've finished reading or viewing to save on storage space. If you are done with a particular book, magazine, or video, you can remove the item from your Fire HD6. (The item remains in your personal space within the Amazon cloud, so you can always download the same item at a later time if you would like to re-read the text.

To remove the item from your Fire HD6, press Home, locate the item on your Home screen, and perform a 'long press' on the icon for the item. From the popup menu that appears, choose 'Remove from Device.'

Chapter 4: Free Books, Movies, and Music Tips, Tricks and Traps

Your Fire HD6 is a great source of reading and entertainment, but let's face it: content costs, and quality contents costs more. Like everyone else, authors and songwriters certainly expect to eat (no surprise there), and production costs skyrocket when you get into the league of big-name entertainers and the costs of producing those Hollywood blockbusters that you're fond of watching on the 'small screen'. But there are great sources of free, quality content available for your Fire. My favorite source is one that in a way, you've likely already paid for (and continue paying for) over the years: I'm speaking of your tax-supported, local public library.

Getting Kindle Books from your local library (without setting foot in your library)

Borrow Kindle content for free from your public library. Many Kindle owners are oblivious to the fact that most public libraries now loan books, movies, music, and other digital content for the Amazon Kindle line of e-readers (as well as for other digital products like smartphones, Apple iPads, and other tablet computers.) In the United States alone, at the time of this writing, nearly 20,000 public libraries are members of a system called OverDrive Media. OverDrive Media provides an app for your Fire HD6 that lets you borrow content electronically from your public library. All you'll need is the app (a free download from the Amazon store) and your library card number. Check with your local library to see if they are a member of the OverDrive program. You should be able to check without getting out of your easy chair; do a Google search for your town's public library web site, and once you find it, look for a link that says "download e-books"

or something similar. If your city does not have a membership in such a program, there are libraries that allow nonresidents to obtain a library card for an annual fee. Two, at the time of this writing, are those of Fairfax County, Virginia (www.fairfaxcounty.gov/library for more information) and the City of Philadelphia (www.freelibrary.org for more information).

Once you've found that your library is a member of the OverDrive Media service, go to the Amazon App store, search on the term 'overdrive', and download the app to your Fire HD6. Launch the app, and you'll be asked for a ZIP code; enter your zip code, and you'll see your local library's name in a list. Select your library by name, and you'll be taken to a page for your local library, where you can borrow books, movies, and other digital content. Browse among what your library has available for lending, click on a title, and you'll be taken to an Amazon page with the book, but in place of the "Buy with one click" button, you'll see a "Borrow from library" button. Click that button, and the book will be downloaded to your Fire.

Different libraries have different lending policies, so you'll want to check with your local library to determine the exact length of your loan. In my resident town of Charlotte, North Carolina, books have a two-week loan with one possible renewal, and movies are good for ten days. Many libraries now offer regularly scheduled classes or workshops that teach library patrons how to download digital content, so you may want to visit your local library and sign up for such a class in your home town.

Using the Kindle Owner's Lending Library ("KOLL") to your advantage

The second great free source of books is Amazon's own Kindle Owners Lending Library. If you are a member of Amazon Prime, you owe it to yourself to check out the Kindle Owners' Lending Library. The Kindle Owners Lending Library allows Amazon Prime members to borrow one book at a time each month, at no cost. There are thousands of books available through the service, and you can find free books to borrow through the Kindle Owners Lending Library using these steps:

1. At the Kindle Fire store, click "See all categories." When the list of various categories (Books, Kindle Singles, Kindle Newsstand, New & Noteworthy, etc.) appears, click the Kindle Owners' Lending Library option.

2. After picking the Kindle Owners' Lending Library, you can browse a list of books to borrow. You will know that a book is eligible for borrowing because it will have a "Prime" badge attached.

3. Click the 'Borrow' tab. Next, you'll see a "Buy for $xx.xx" tab and a "Borrow for Free" tab. Click the "Borrow for Free" tab, and your borrowed book will be downloaded to your Fire.

Easily Search the Kindle Store on your Fire for Free Books

A third great way to find free books is to search for... free books! As part of regular ongoing promotions, many authors will place their books on sale for nothing during certain days of a 90-day period, as part of an authors' program called Amazon KDP Select. You can take advantage of this fact by simply searching among any desired genre of Kindle books, and entering "0.00" as your search criteria in the Search box. What appears will be every Kindle book that has a price of zero dollars, zero cents on that particular day. (And before you think that checking this list would result in a limited selection, you should know that on any given day there are hundreds of free books offered through Amazon's promotional program.) This list of books will change wildly on a daily basis, so if you're an avid reader, you may find it worth your while to perform this sort of a search on a regular basis.

Download free books from the Internet, and transfer these to your Fire HD6 using your USB cable. The final source of free books that this chapter will detail is that of the Internet itself. You can find countless sources of free e-books on the Internet. These come in a variety of file formats; besides its own native file format of Kindle (.azw) files, your Fire HD6 will also read books in Adobe Acrobat (.PDF) format, in MobiPocket (.MOBI) format, or in plain text (.TXT) format. Unfortunately, your Fire HD6 will NOT read files in the popular E-PUB format used by the Sony e-reader, the Barnes and Noble NOOK, and many other e-readers. The solution for this is not overwhelmingly complex; you can download free e-book converter programs that will convert e-books from most other formats into Amazon's Kindle (.KZW) format. An excellent program is called Calibre (go to www.calibre-ebook.com for details). Calibre can convert files from many formats, including the E-PUB format, into the Amazon Kindle file format. Once you convert the file, use the file transfer techniques described in Chapter 5 of this book, to transfer the e-books that you've converted to your Fire HD6.

As for sources, performing a Google search for "free e-books" will return an avalanche of sites. Here is a small list to get you started:

Project Gutenberg- www.gutenberg.org

ManyBooks.net- http://manybooks.net

Google Books- http://books.google.com/

MobiPocket Free Books- www.mobipocket.com/freebooks/

An exhaustive source of free computer-based books can be found at http://freecomputerbooks.com. Finally, you'll find a surprisingly comprehensive list of textbooks that can be legally shared, at http://textbookrevolution.org. These are in .PDF format.

Get free movies and TV shows with your Prime membership

If you are a major fan of watching movies and television shows or you are a fan of streaming music, the author has a recommendation for you. Consider becoming a member of Amazon Prime, if you aren't already a member. For an annual fee of under $100 (at the time of this writing), in addition to the free two day shipping on a variety of items, you will also get to watch thousands of movies and shows from the Amazon Prime video library on your Fire at no cost. Prime members can stream from a selection of thousands of movies and shows.

Your yearly subscription to Amazon Prime includes free unlimited access to thousands of movies and TV shows from Amazon Prime Instant Video, part of Amazon's own video streaming service. Note that there is Amazon Prime Instant Video and there is Amazon Instant Video, and the two aren't exactly the same. Amazon Instant Video is Amazon's video streaming service, with tens of thousands of movies and TV shows available for rent or purchase at various prices. Amazon Prime Instant Video is the library of all Amazon

Instant Video content that happens to be free to Amazon Prime members. You can tell whether a video is free with your Prime membership by looking for the "Prime" banner at the upper-left corner, as shown in the following example:

To quickly browse what's available when you're a Prime member, at the Home Screen, tap 'Videos' in the main menu, then navigate to and tap a Prime-related subcategory—Recently Added to Prime, Top Movies in Prime Instant Videos, or Kids Movies in Prime Instant Videos (for movies), or Top TV in Prime Instant Videos and Kids TV in Prime Instant Videos (for TV shows). Once you have a subcategory selected, you can swipe left or right to locate a desired movie or show within that category, and tap the movie or TV show to begin watching.

Getting free music with Prime Music

When you are a Prime subscriber, you also receive the benefit of no-cost access to Amazon Prime Music. With Amazon Prime Music, you can listen to your choice of songs from a library of over one million songs. You can choose individual songs, entire albums, or customized playlists created by Amazon's music experts. You can also create your own playlists, and best of all, you can download songs of your choosing to your Fire so that you can listen later, even when you are off-line.

To get to Prime Music, go to the Home screen, and then tap "Music" in the menu bar. At the next screen that appears, tap Prime Music. This will take you to the Prime Music screen, shown here:

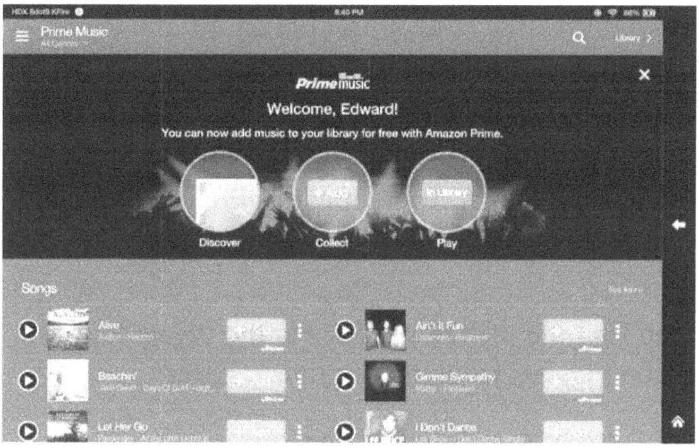

To listen to songs from Prime Music, at the Home screen, tap Music to navigate to your music library and browse or search by playlists, artists, albums, songs, or genres. Choose a song, album, or playlist and tap Play to begin playing the song, album, or playlist.

Creating a playlist

You can create playlists that contain your favorite songs using the following steps:

1. Click the check boxes next to the songs you want to add to the playlist.

2. Click "Add to playlist."

3. Click "New playlist" from the drop-down list that appears on the screen to create a new playlist.

Downloading Prime Music for Offline Playback

On any Amazon Fire, as well as phones and other tablets with the Amazon Music app installed, Prime members can also download Prime Music (including Prime Playlists) for offline playback. You can use these steps to download Prime Music for offline playback:

1. Add the Prime Music you want to download to your music library.

2. Search or browse your music library for the Prime song, album, or playlist you want to download.

3. On a Fire or on an Android tablet, press and hold the title you want to download, and then choose Download from the menu that appears. On an Apple iPad or iPhone, swipe the songs you want to download, tap More, and then tap Download.

You can find the offline versions in the Prime Playlists section under the Playlist view in your music library.

Licensing Limitations of Prime Music

Prime Music is available for streaming on only one device at a time, for each Amazon account. Prime Music is available to download (for offline playback) to only four devices at a time, for each Amazon account. If you try to download Prime Music to an additional device, you will be asked to (1)-start the download on that device (and automatically deactivate the Prime Music that you downloaded to your least recently used device), or (2)-leave your active device settings unchanged. Finally, due to music licensing agreements, Prime Music is (at the time of this writing) limited to Amazon customers having a US or Puerto Rico mailing address, with the account billed to a financial institution based in the US or Puerto Rico.

Have music, will travel...

Keep in mind that your Fire isn't the only way in which you can enjoy Prime music. In addition to using your Fire, you can also use the Amazon Music App on any compatible platform. The Amazon Music App is available for nearly all Android phones and tablets, and Apple iOS devices including the iPhone and iPad lines. To download the app, go to the respective app store for your device (such as the Google

PlayStore for an Android phone), and search on the term "Amazon music app."

About Kindle Unlimited, a Subscription Service that offers unlimited reading of select Amazon titles

The final option mentioned in this chapter (because you are in effect paying a monthly fee to read any of hundreds of thousands of titles) is Amazon's own Kindle Unlimited subscription service. In a nutshell, you give Amazon $10.00 each month, and in return, the company gives you no-cost access to a library of over 600,000 titles. For 10 bucks per month, it's "read all you want." Kindle Unlimited appears to be a close relative to Amazon Prime Music. Both services ask the question, "Why buy content that costs every time you download that content, when you can pay one monthly fee to rent as much content as you want?"(If you are familiar with Netflix, the popular streaming video service, it may be helpful to think of Kindle Unlimited as a "Netflix for books.")

It may be helpful, when deciding whether to choose Kindle Unlimited or not to choose Kindle Unlimited, to realize that you are making a decision in the classic "rent vs. buy" quandary. The following paragraphs cover a number of things that you should know before signing up for Kindle Unlimited:

1. The Kindle Unlimited library will not give you access to many of the latest bestsellers.

2. Kindle Unlimited is a rental service, which means that you rent, and do not own, the books. As long as you are enrolled in the Kindle Unlimited service, you have access to the books within the Kindle Unlimited library. If you were to end your subscription, the books that had been checked out of the Kindle Unlimited library would be available only until the end of the current billing cycle. Also, you would not be able to access any more books from the Kindle Unlimited library. This loss of access upon termination of your Kindle Unlimited

subscription applies to all books taken from the Kindle Unlimited library, including audible books.

3. Your subscription to Kindle Unlimited is a monthly subscription, and it automatically renews each month, unless you manually turn off the auto-renewal option. (You will need to do this if at any time you decide to cancel your membership. If you decide to cancel membership, note that you will not receive a refund of any amount already billed to your Amazon account.)

4. To sign up for Kindle Unlimited, you must have an Amazon account, your account must have payments enabled with a valid credit card, and you must also have the “1-click payment” option turned on.

5. At the time of this writing, Kindle Unlimited is only available to customers in the United States or Puerto Rico, and your credit or debit card used for billing must be issued by a bank based in the US or Puerto Rico.

So, is a Kindle Unlimited subscription a wise choice for you? The answer to this question is, "it depends." An excellent first question to ask yourself is, "do I read more than one book per month?" If you typically read just one book per month (or less), then Kindle Unlimited is likely not a program that makes sense for you. If you purchase two or more books each month, you may want to take a look at the Kindle Unlimited program.

This kind of comparison makes sense, assuming you are the type of reader who has been reading paperback or hardcover books, and you are now in the process of making the jump to digital books. If you've been reading your books on a Kindle or iPad in the past, then you know you've already seen large savings over those who still buy paper-based books. As an example, my sister reads an average of 3 to 5 books each month. But I'm not convinced that she would benefit from Amazon's Kindle Unlimited, because she tends to pick and choose from the New York Times bestseller list. At the time this analysis was written, I consulted the current New York

Times bestseller list, then checked to see how many books on the New York Times bestseller list were also available on Kindle Unlimited, and I came up with a total of just ***six titles***. My spouse, on the other hand, reads a lot of sci-fi/fantasy, particularly by new and up and coming "indie" authors. Because many of these authors self-publish through Amazon and tend to promote their books using KDP Select, finding a wide assortment of books within this genre at Kindle Unlimited is a simple matter. You should examine the possible selections under the Kindle Unlimited program and analyze your own reading habits before spending the monthly subscription fee.

Chapter 5: Silk browser tips, tricks, and traps

The Amazon Silk web browser for the Fire is unique among web browsers, engineered from the ground up especially for the Fire. Since Android-based tablets will certainly run established browsers such as Google Chrome and Mozilla Firefox, many have wondered why Amazon chose to design a new browser from scratch. The answer is, Amazon wanted to offer a fast browsing experience, so the browser design splits tasks between the browser software that is running locally on the Fire, and Amazon's Cloud Servers. As a result of this unique design, a number of features are familiar to you because you've seen them in other browsers, but there are a few that are unique to the Silk browser.

Surfing the Web with the Silk Browser

To launch the Silk browser, at the Home screen, finger-swipe the Navigation bar near the top to the far right and tap Web, or tap the Silk Browser icon within the carousel (it resembles the following):

. Tap the icon or tap Web' in the Navigation bar, and (assuming you have an active Internet connection) the Silk browser opens to the web page for the last site you visited. The following illustration shows the parts of the Silk browser.

The Silk browser is a tabbed browser, like Google's Chrome, Mozilla Firefox, and more recent versions of Microsoft Internet Explorer. To open a new tab, just tap the plus sign in the top right corner. You can then tap in the Search field and enter the desired web address.

Quick access to the Quick Menu

The Silk browser has a number of options and settings that can be reached from the Quick menu. And with the Fire HD6 and HD7 models comes a new way to get there. If you press and swipe from the left edge of the device (just outside the visible screen area) out to the right, you will drag open the Silk browser's Quick menu, shown in the following illustration. (You can also tap the three horizontal lines at the upper-left corner.)

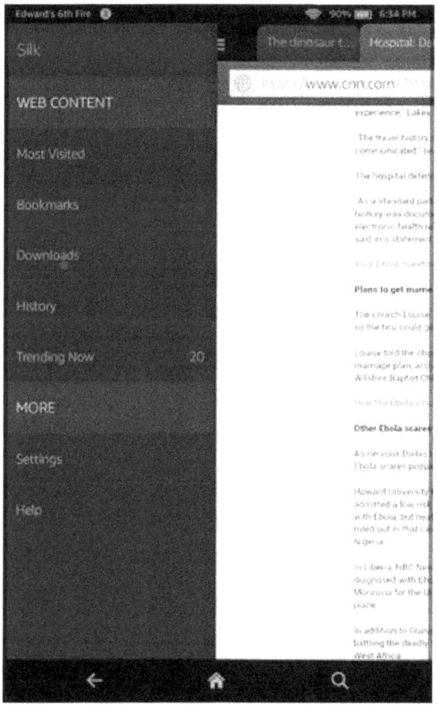

From here, you can access your bookmarks, history of recently-visited pages, downloads, and pages that are "trending now" across the web. You can also access the Settings page which offers various ways to customize the settings of the Silk browser, as explained in later parts of this chapter.

If you are viewing a page and there is a link embedded in the page and you would like to go to that link in a separate tab, give the link a long press rather than a tap. A menu of options will appear, and you can choose 'Open in new tab' from the menu.

Share web pages with your friends. When a page is displayed in the Silk browser, the Quick menu icon (three vertical dots) at the bottom of the browser window will include a Share Page symbol. Tap this symbol, and you can send a link to the page either via email, or through Facebook or Twitter.

The "thumb and finger spread" or "thumb and finger pinch" works in the Silk browser. You will often encounter web pages with text that is too small to read on the Fire screen. Place your thumb and finger on the screen and spread them to magnify, or pinch them together to reduce the magnification.

Use "Find on this page" as a search tool. Oftentimes you will need to search a website for a particular word or phrase. To do this in the Silk browser, tap the quick menu icon (three vertical dots) at the bottom of the window, then tap "Find in page." Enter a search term in the search field that appears, and use the up and down arrow keys to move through the search results.

Let the browser complete your entry. As you begin typing characters into the search / address field, a list of suggestions appears below the field. Type more characters, and suggestions increase in accuracy. When you see a suggestion that matches the URL you intended to type, tap that suggestion.

Using Bookmarks

Bookmark commonly visited pages so you can return to them quickly at a later time. As with all modern web browsers, the Silk browser provides the ability to bookmark sites so that you can easily return to the same site. To add a bookmark, tap the Quick Menu icon at the bottom of the browser window then tap Add Bookmark. You will now see the Add Bookmarks dialog box. Change the name of the entry to something friendlier if you desire, and tap OK, to add the page to your bookmarked pages.

Quickly get to your bookmarked pages. There are different ways to go to a bookmarked page, but this method seems to involve the least amount of steps. Press at the left edge of the screen and swipe to the right, to drag the Silk sidebar out. Tap Bookmarks, locate the desired bookmark, and tap the desired bookmark to open it in the current page. (You can also perform a long press on the desired bookmark, and choose Open in New Tab from the menu that appears to open the webpage in a new tab.)

Delete any bookmark page that's no longer needed. From the Bookmarks page (get there by tapping the Menu icon at the top left, or by pressing and swiping out from the left edge of the screen, and tapping Bookmarks), perform a long-press on the unwanted bookmark, and choose "Delete" from the menu that appears.

Changing Silk Settings for Best Operation

Choose your preferred search engine. The default search engine for the Silk browser is Microsoft Bing, but if you prefer to use Google or Yahoo as your default search engine, you can change the Silk browser to either of these options. Tap the menu icon at the upper left corner or press at the left edge and swipe outwards, tap Settings, tap Search Engine, and make your desired choice.

Keep Silk performance up through regular housecleaning. Just as browsers on your PC can be slowed over time from too many cookies or from a clogged cache, so can the Silk browser. You can perform a bit of browser housecleaning on occasion; to do so, tap the menu icon at the upper left corner or press at the left edge and swipe outwards, tap Settings, and tap the Clear Browser Data option.

Set your Silk settings to your preferences. The Silk browser has a number of settings that you can use to change the operation of the browser. Tap the menu icon at the upper left corner or press at the left edge and swipe outwards, and then tap Settings. You will see the settings that apply to the browser, as shown in the following illustration.

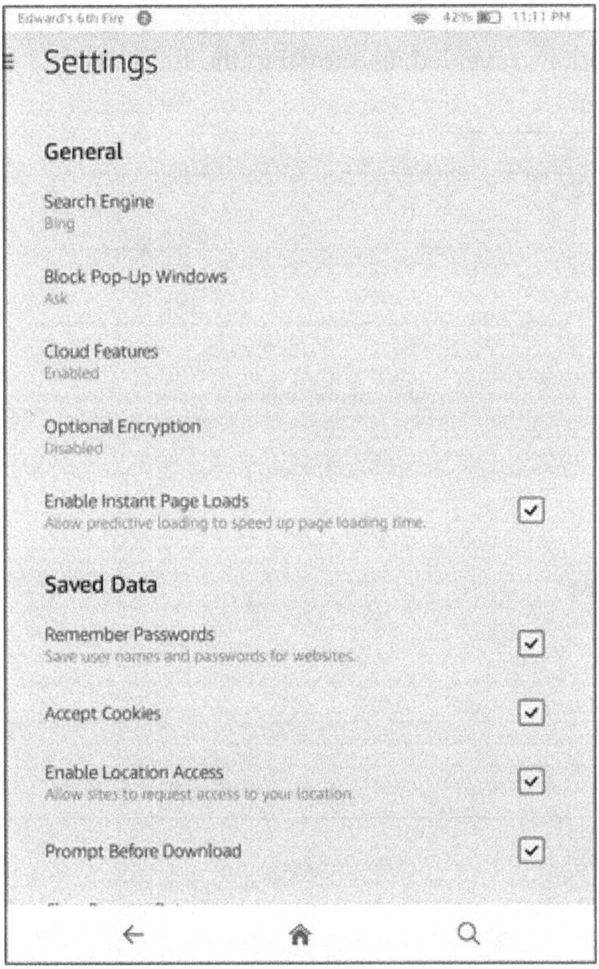

(Silk browser settings)

These settings affect the way the Silk Browser behaves in various ways. Under Search Engine, you can specify the desired search engine used by the browser, and you can choose to block popup windows and whether to enable cloud-based features of the Amazon Cloud. The Enable Instant Page Loads option is by default set to on; however you may wish to consider turning off this option if the types of websites that you visit appear to be hampered by predictive page loading.

If you scroll down in the Silk Settings screen, you will see additional options revealed, as shown in the following illustration.

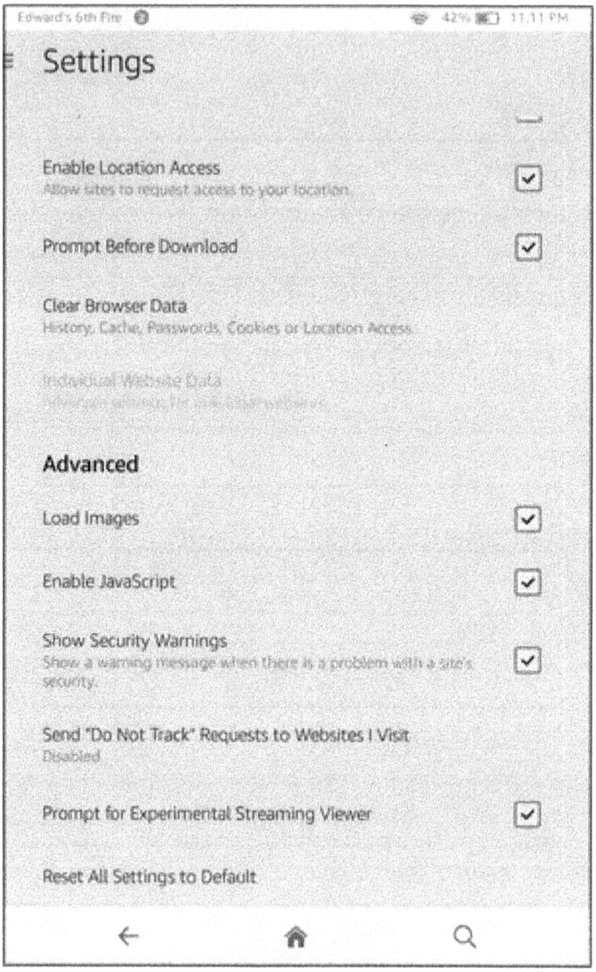

These options include whether or not you want to clear browser data (the history, the cache, and all cookie data) from the browser. You also have options to remember passwords used when visiting sites, to clear all passwords from the browser memory, and whether or not cookies should be accepted by the browser. You can enable location tracking or clear location access, and under Advanced Settings, you can choose whether images are normally loaded, whether

JavaScript is enabled, and whether security warnings are enabled.

Chapter 6: File Management Tips, Tricks, and Traps

In press reviews, the Fire has taken a fair share of criticism for being a relatively "closed ecosystem," according to its critics. Many reviewers have claimed that Fire owners are dependent on purchasing virtually all content from Amazon. In the opinion of this author, that reputation is somewhat undeserved. Certainly, it is in Amazon's interest to get you to buy your content from Amazon. But the 'closed ecosystem' claim made by many members of the press implies that you must purchase all your content from Amazon, and that is simply not the case. In addition to purchasing content from the Amazon store, you can find millions (literally!) of books from other sources, and these can be copied to your Fire from your computer using the USB cable that is a part of your charging assembly. The Fire uses the .mobi file format for its e-books, and e-books in the .mobi format can be found in thousands of places all over the internet, some paid, and others free. There are also millions of books in the popular E-PUB format used by Sony and by Google, and there are free converters readily available from hundreds of sources on the web that will convert files from the E-PUB format into the .mobi format used by all Amazon Kindles.

You can use the same USB cable techniques to copy MP3, AAC, or WAV files that you obtain from your own sources, and these become a part of the music library on your Fire. There are apps like Crackle that let you stream any one of thousands of free movies or TV shows to your Fire. If you are already a Netflix subscriber, you can download the Netflix app from the Amazon app store (the app is free) and watch any content that you would normally obtain from Netflix on your Fire. And short length, personal movies compatible with the Fire (in 3gp or mp4 format) can also be copied to the device, although the 8 gigabyte memory size is by nature going to limit the length of movies that can be stored locally on the device. (By comparison, an average Blu-ray DVD occupies 25 gigabytes of disk space.)

You can also email documents directly to your Fire, using Amazon's free Send to Kindle service. Every registered Kindle has its own assigned email address, and you can send certain types of files- Microsoft Word documents, rich text (RTF) or text (TXT) files, .JPG or .PNG graphics files, Adobe PDF files, and others- to your Fire's assigned email address. (See the following heading if you do not know your Fire's assigned e-mail address.) Within roughly 5 minutes of the time that you send a file as an attachment, it will show up on your Fire, in the Documents folder. You can then tap the document to open it and read it in the native Kindle Viewer, and there are apps available that will let you edit Microsoft Word documents on your Kindle.

To take full advantage of all of these features of the Fire, you'll need to know how to use the file management features of the Fire. You'll find the various tips, tricks, and traps that pertain to these topics covered throughout this chapter.

Sending Files to your Fire via E-mail

Know your Fire's email address. If you purchased your Fire directly from Amazon, it was registered for you when it arrived. If you purchased it from a retailer such as Best Buy, you may have gone through the setup steps on your own. In either case, your Fire has been assigned a Send to Kindle email address. This address is something similar to ***username@kindle.com***. To see your email address, pull down the Navigation bar, tap Settings, and under Settings, tap My Account. You will see a message that reads something like-

Edward's second Kindle is registered to Edward Jones edjones45@kindle.com

This is the email address that you can use to send files as attachments to your Fire.

Before you can send any documents to your Fire, you must add the sending email address to an "Approved personal document email list" under your Amazon account settings. To prevent Fire owners from receiving unwanted spam, Amazon blocks any email sent to a Kindle address at Kindle.com that hasn't been added to the approved personal document email list. Log into your Amazon account in a computer's web browser, and under the 'Your Account' link, click 'Manage Your Device.' At the next screen that appears, you'll see all your Amazon devices (assuming you own more than one). If you own just one Fire HD6, you will see just that device. Scroll down and locate the desired Fire in your list of devices, click the Edit link to the right of the device name, and you will be able to change the e-mail address registered to that Fire. You can also add authorized e-mail addresses that will be permitted to send e-mail to your Fire. By default, Amazon adds the e-mail address that is associated with your Amazon account. To add authorized addresses, under 'Your Kindle Account' at the left, click Personal Document Settings, then look for the Approved Personal Document E-mail List near the bottom of the screen. You can click the 'Add a new Approved E-mail Address' link in this area to add another email address.

Once you've added your email address to the approved personal document email list, you can

attach files to an email message and send it to your send to kindle address. Documents can be in the form of .DOC, .DOCX, .RTF, .TXT, .HTM or .HTML, ZIP, .MOBI' and .AZW file formats. Images can be sent in the .JPG, .PNG, .GIF, or .BMP file formats. The conversion process assumes an active wi-fi connection, since Amazon's Send to Kindle service converts your file into Amazon's own .AZW file format, then downloads it to your Fire using Amazon's Whispernet.

Attachments cannot be larger than 50 megabytes per attachment, and each email must not have more than 25 attachments. If any of your files are larger than 50 megabytes, the Send to Kindle process will fail for that file, and that file will not appear in your Documents folder.

Use the Send to Kindle service to convert PDF files to Amazon readable documents. In addition to the file types listed in the previous tip, you can also send PDF files to your Kindle, and Amazon uses a conversion service to convert the PDF file into Amazon's own .AZW file format. Simply add the word "convert" to the subject line of your email, then attach the PDF file and send the email to your Send to Kindle email address.

Transferring Files to your Fire with its Charging Cable

You can also transfer files from a laptop or desktop computer to your Fire, using a USB to micro-USB cable. This is the same type of cable that is supplied as a charging cable for your Fire; one end contains the micro USB connector that plugs into the base of your Fire, and the other end contains a standard USB connector. Use the cable to connect your Fire to your computer, and the Fire will appear as a USB flash drive under your computer's operating system.

Users of Windows XP may have to install additional software before using a USB cable to access the Fire, and the users of the Apple Mac will have to install additional software. Go to the following link for additional details:

http://www.kindle.com/support/downloads

Once the Fire appears as a USB drive under your computer's operating system, you can simply drag and drop or copy and paste the desired files into the appropriate folders of the Fire.

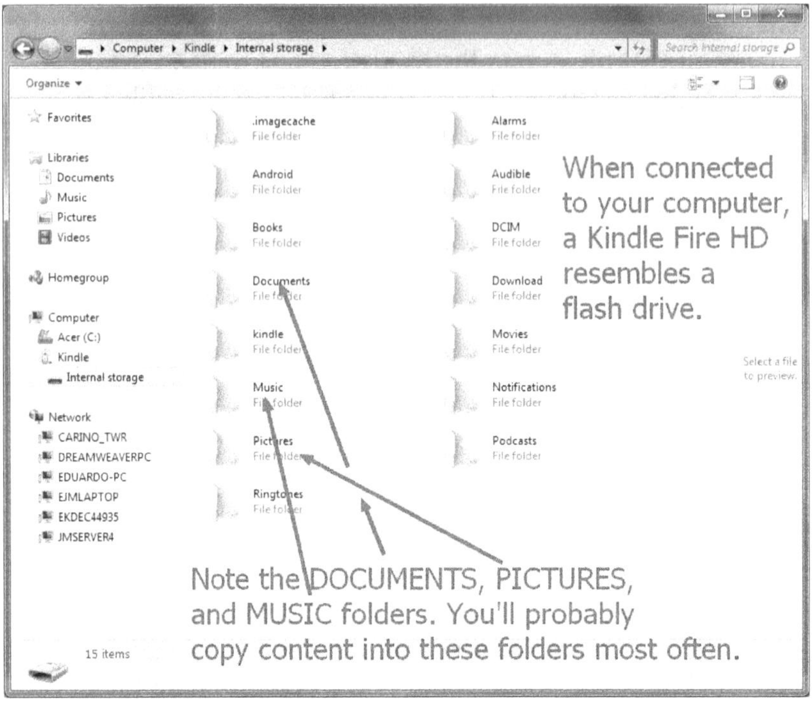

You can use a USB cable to transfer files in the form of .DOC, .DOCX, .XLS, .PPT, .RTF, .TXT, .HTM or .HTML, ZIP, .MOBI' and .AZW file formats. Images can be in the .JPG, .PNG, .GIF, or .BMP file formats, and audio files can be in the .AAC, .MP3, .MIDI, .OGG, or .WAV file formats.

The built in file viewer that is included with your Fire will allow you to open and view files in the common Microsoft office formats, but you will not be able to edit these files. If you wish to edit these files, there are apps available from the Amazon app store that will let you edit Microsoft Office files. The author happens to like QuickOffice Pro, which is priced at a cost of just under $10.00 at the time of this writing, and there are other similar apps, including Kingsoft Office by Kingsoft, and Documents to Go by DataWiz.

Transferring Files Wirelessly with the Wi-Fi File Explorer App

You can transfer files to your Fire HD6 wirelessly ('look ma, no cables!') Assuming you have a home network with PCs attached to it, you don't necessarily have to resort to the annoyance of a cable connected between your Fire and your computer every time you want to move a file between the two. Wi-Fi File Explorer is a neat little app that lets you transfer files wirelessly. Download and install this free app on your Fire, and when you run the app, once you identify the wi-fi network used by the Fire, you'll see a display giving you a web address that you can point a browser on any computer that's also on your network. The address will include a port number, similar to the following:

http://192.168.1.15:8000

Point your computer's web browser to the address you're given (yours will likely differ from this example) and you'll see a display like the following:

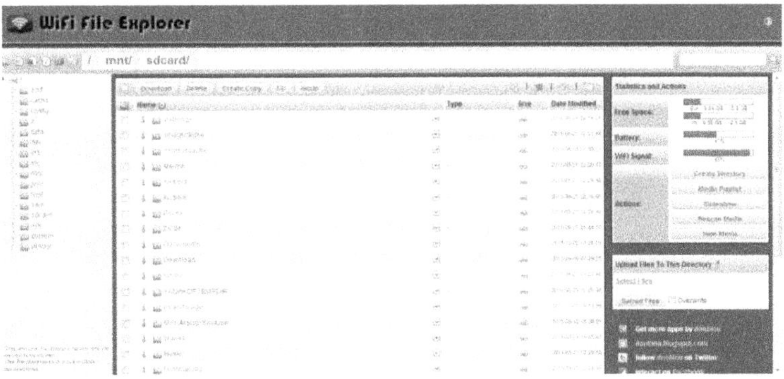

Wi-Fi File Explorer gives you a file explorer view of all the folders on your Fire HD6. You can drill down into any folder, and use the Download button at the top of the Wi-Fi File Explorer window to move files from your laptop to your Fire, without the hassle of wires.

Chapter 7: Email Tips, Tricks, and Traps

One of the many capabilities of the Fire centers on the email client that is built into the device. All of the basic features that you would expect to find in an email client are here; you can open and read mail, reply to and compose mail, download attachments, and send email with attached files. The HD6 model of the Fire adds significant improvements to the built-in e-mail client. Clearly Amazon engineering has been paying attention to user feedback, because the e-mail client that was mediocre at best in the first generation Fires has improved to a level of capable, in this author's opinion. The e-mail app now supports labeling, threaded conversations, and archiving of emails for offline reading. Integrated calendar support of both Google's Gmail and Microsoft Exchange are additional welcome features. Tips, tricks, and traps dealing with email are covered in this chapter.

Setting up your Fire HD6 E-mail

Set up an email account quickly with Auto-configuration. If you're like many individuals, you probably have a number of e-mail accounts. With your Fire HD6, you can stay on top of your e-mail from anywhere. Later sections of this chapter will delve into using e-mail on the Fire HD6 in greater detail, but for now, you may find the great auto-configuration feature is all you need to get your multiple e-mail accounts up and running. The feature works with e-mail accounts provided by Google (Gmail), Yahoo Mail, AOL Mail, Microsoft Live Mail (formerly known as Hotmail), Microsoft's Outlook.com, Apple's iCloud Mail, and BT Internet (United Kingdom). Use the following steps to set up your e-mail account on your Fire HD6:

1. From the Home screen, tap Apps in the Navigation bar. When your Apps screen appears, tap 'Device' at the upper right to see the apps on your device, then tap the Email app. Assuming you've never setup an email account on your Fire, the Add Account screen will appear, as shown in the following illustration. (If an e-mail account has been set up on your device and you want to add another, drag down the Navigation bar from the top of the screen, and tap Settings > Applications >Email, Contacts, Calendar > Add Account.)

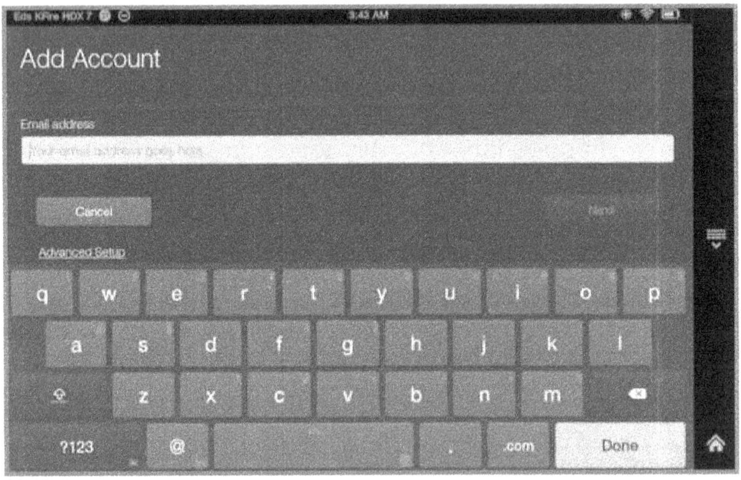

Enter your e-mail address and then tap Next. You will now see a sign-in screen for Google, Yahoo, AOL, Microsoft Live or Outlook Mail, depending on your choice of e-mail providers, or you may see a screen asking for your password. (An example of the sign-in screen presented to users of Google's Gmail is shown in the following illustration.)

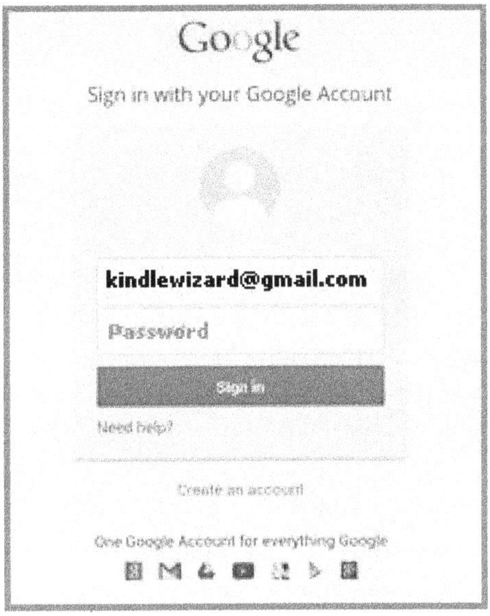

Enter the requested information, and your Fire will attempt to connect the new email account settings with the servers of your email account provider. Once it successfully does so, you'll see a synchronization options screen, similar to the one shown in the following illustration:

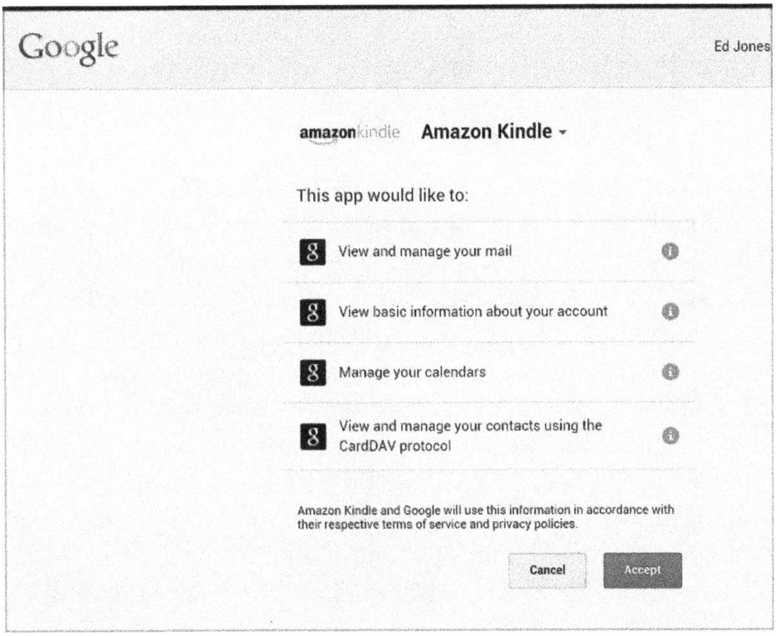

This screen asks for permission to synchronize your contacts and calendar on your Fire HD6 with that of your e-mail provider. Tap Accept, and in a moment, you should see a screen indicating a successful setup of your e-mail account.

Fire receives incoming emails, but is unable to send outgoing emails. After setup of an email account, some users report that they are able to receive emails, but can't send mail. The problem is usually that when you fill in the setup screen, the Fire assumes that your username is also your outgoing SMTP address setting. And this is true with most providers, but not with all providers. As an example, if your email provider is Comcast cable, and your full email address is ***johndoe@comcast.net***, when going through the setup screen, you probably entered ***johndoe*** when prompted for a user name. As a result, the Fire's email client is trying to send out email with an SMTP address setting of ***johndoe***, when the setting should be ***johndoe@comcast.net***. To solve the problem, go back into the email settings you have on your Fire, and enter the entire outgoing email address manually. (For details on how to do this, see the following topic.)

Setting up e-mail manually

The automated e-mail setup on the Fire HD6 does a great job when it works, but it does not always work, and when it fails to work, you'll need to set up your e-mail manually. Before starting a manual e-mail account setup process, there is some information that you will want to make sure that you have from your e-mail service provider. Of course, you will need to know your e-mail address and the password for the account. In addition, you will need to know the server settings of your mail server. You will need the SMTP settings, as well as either the POP or the IMAP settings. (The SMTP setting is used for sending mail, and POP and IMAP are both used for receiving mail. IMAP is a newer standard for receiving mail, so if your mail server supports both POP and IMAP, use the IMAP settings.) Finally, you will need to know the security type used by the servers, and the default incoming and outgoing ports. (You should be able to obtain all of this information from your e-mail provider.) Once you've obtained the information, perform the following steps to manually set up an e-mail account on the Fire HD6:

1. If no e-mail accounts currently exist on your device, tap Apps, then tap the E-mail icon, and when the next screen appears, tap Create E-mail account. If one or more e-mail accounts already exist on your device, drag down the Navigation bar and tap Settings, and then tap Applications > Email, Contacts, Calendar.

2. At the next screen that appears, tap Add Account.

3. Enter your e-mail address and password where prompted, and then tap Next. You will see an Add Account screen asking you to choose the type of account, as shown in the following illustration.

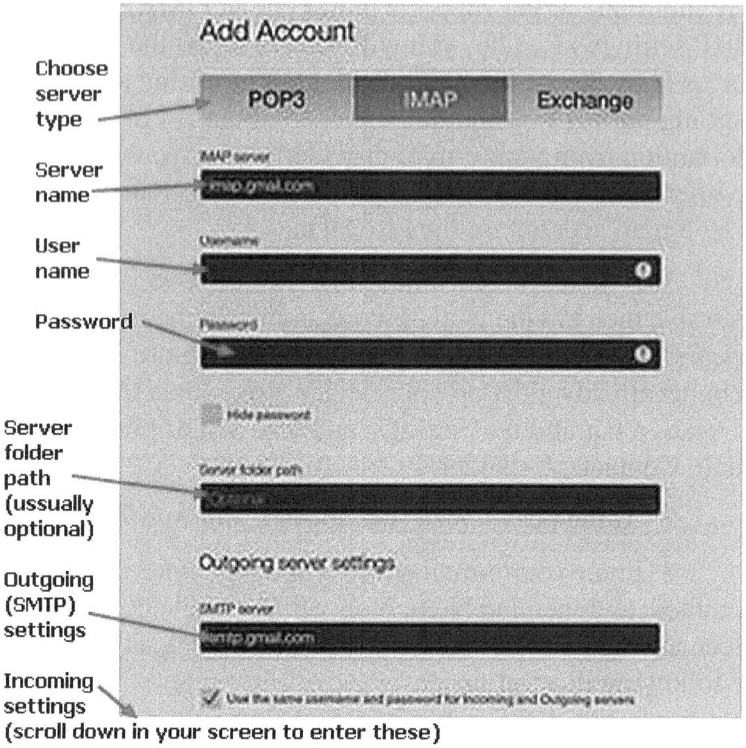

4. Select the type of email account you are creating. (Your available choices are a POP3 account, an IMAP account, or a Microsoft Exchange Account. The remainder of this topic will help you with the common POP3 and IMAP types; if you are setting up a Microsoft Exchange-hosted account, see the following topic for details.

5. Next, you will be asked to provide your incoming server settings. These will include your user name, password, POP3 or IMAP server address, security type, port number, and the desired 'delete email from server' setting. Enter this information, then tap Done at the bottom of the screen.

Your Fire HD6 will attempt to connect to the Incoming server with the settings you supplied. If the connection is successful, the Outgoing server settings screen will appear.

6. Enter your outgoing server settings. These will include your user name, password, SMTP server address, security type (if any), port number, and whether the server will require a sign-in. After entering this information, tap Next.

The first time you connect, you will be asked to give this mail account a unique on-screen name, and you will need to supply your name. (The e-mail app uses the unique account name to differentiate the account from all other email accounts on your Fire HD6.) Touch Done, and your manually created e-mail account is ready for use.

NOTE: Manual setups of e-mail accounts can be tricky, to say the least. You are required to enter a number of values, and if any single value is incorrect, your e-mail works partially, or does no work at all. If you are unsuccessful in setting up your e-mail account, try changing the entry in the 'username' field to your full e-mail address. Some systems expect to see your full e-mail address (such as 'johndoe@carolinarr.timewarnercable.com'), and other systems only want to see the username ('such as 'johndoe'). If you've tried both formats with no success, it's probably time to get as many details about the settings as possible from your e-mail provider, and then punch that 'Help' button on your Fire HD6, and find the current phone number for Amazon technical support.

Setting up E-mail with Microsoft Exchange

Create a Microsoft Exchange e-mail account on the Fire HD6 (if you are using Exchange). In the business world, one of the most commonly-used sources of e-mail is Microsoft's Exchange, a server-based messaging system used by thousands of companies and organizations worldwide. Exchange is offered both as a hardware-and-software based solution that is typically installed and managed by an organization's IT staff, or as a cloud-based solution (as is the case with Microsoft's Office 365, a subscription-based service offered by Microsoft). In either case, if Microsoft Exchange is the provider of e-mail, contacts, and calendaring at your office, the good news is that you can set up your Fire HD6 to access your e-mail, contacts, and calendar that are hosted by Microsoft Exchange. The Fire HD6 sports major improvements to the operating system that make an Exchange e-mail account setup much simpler than on earlier generation Kindle Fires. You'll want to turn on your Fire HD6 and ensure that you have an active Wi-Fi connection. Once this is done, you can perform the following steps to set up e-mail, contacts, and calendaring from Microsoft Exchange on your Fire HD6:

1. If no e-mail accounts currently exist on your device, tap Apps, then tap the E-mail icon, and when the next screen appears, tap Create E-mail account. If one or more e-mail accounts already exist on your device, drag down the Navigation bar and tap Settings, and then tap Applications > Email, Contacts, Calendar.

2. At the next screen that appears, tap Add Account.

3. Enter your e-mail address and password where prompted, and then click Done. You will now see an Add Account screen asking you to choose the type of account, as shown in the following illustration.

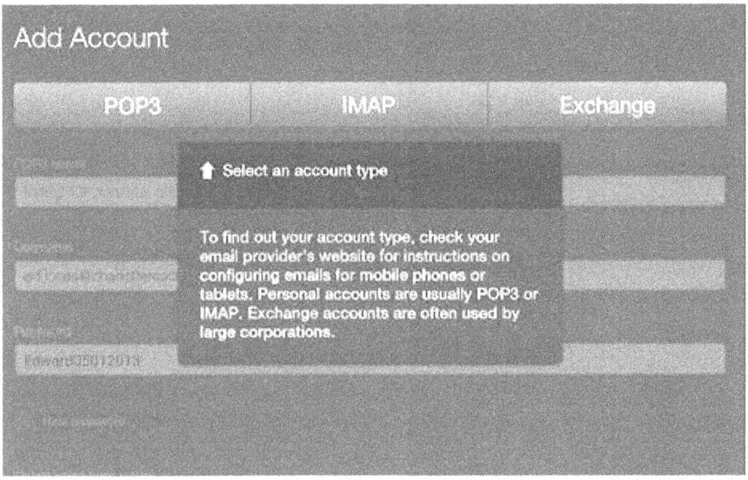

4. At the top of this screen, tap Exchange. The next screen that you see, shown in the following illustration, asks you for the settings that apply to your Microsoft Exchange server. These include the server name, your username and password on the Exchange server, the server's Domain name (often optional), and the security settings and ports used by the server.

In the Exchange server field, enter the name of your Exchange server. If you're connecting to a Microsoft cloud-based Office 365 email account, the Exchange server name will be **`outlook.office365.com`**. If you are using a web-hosted Exchange account provided by a web hosting service like 1and1 Internet or GoDaddy.com, your hosting provider will be able to provide you with this information. If you're not using Office 365 or a web-hosted Exchange account, contact the Exchange server administrator at your organization's I.T. department for the name of your Exchange server.

Under Username, enter your full email address, and in the Password field, make sure your password is correct, then click Done.

The Domain field will contain the word, 'Optional.' Unless a domain name has been given to you by a web-based hosting provider or by your organization's I.T. department, you can leave this field empty.

If your web-based hosting provider or by your organization's I.T. department has provided you with security settings and /or port settings needed by your Exchange server, click the 'Security Settings and Ports' link beneath the 'Domain' field. This will result in the display of another screen, asking about secure connections (SSL) options and port settings. Enter the details given by your email provider, and click Save.

You may see a Remote security administration notice that reads, "The server <Your Exchange Server Name> requires that you allow it to remotely control some security features on your device. Do you want to finish setting up this account?" If this notice appears, tap OK.

Finally, you will see a screen bearing the descriptive name of your e-mail account, along with synchronization options for synchronizing your contacts and calendar on the Exchange server with the contacts and calendar on your Fire. Turn on the Contacts and Calendar checkboxes as desired, to specify whether or not you want to synchronize your contacts and calendar items between Microsoft Exchange and your Fire HD6. After making your selections, tap Save. (Note that by default, your e-mail will be synchronized between the e-mail account on the Fire HD6 and the e-mail account under

Microsoft Exchange; you cannot turn off e-mail synchronization.)

After tapping Save, a 'Setup complete!' screen appears, and you can tap View Inbox to access your Exchange-based email on your Fire HD6.

Reading your E-Mail

The e-mail client that is provided with your Fire does all that you would expect of a solid e-mail client. You can read, compose, and send emails, and you can add attachments to those emails. You can also read e-mails that contain attachments of many file types, including pictures, video attachments, Adobe .PDF attachments, and Microsoft office document attachments. The e-mail client also integrates with the Contacts app that is built into the Fire HD6, so you can send e-mails to contacts that you enter in your contacts directory.

You perform most common mail-related tasks from your Inbox. To get to your Inbox, tap Apps, then locate and tap the Email icon. Your Inbox opens, displaying your mail in a fashion similar to that shown here, assuming that you are in landscape view. (If you are in portrait view, you will only see either the message list or the contents of the message at one time, so you may want to switch to landscape view for best reading by rotating the Fire HD6.)

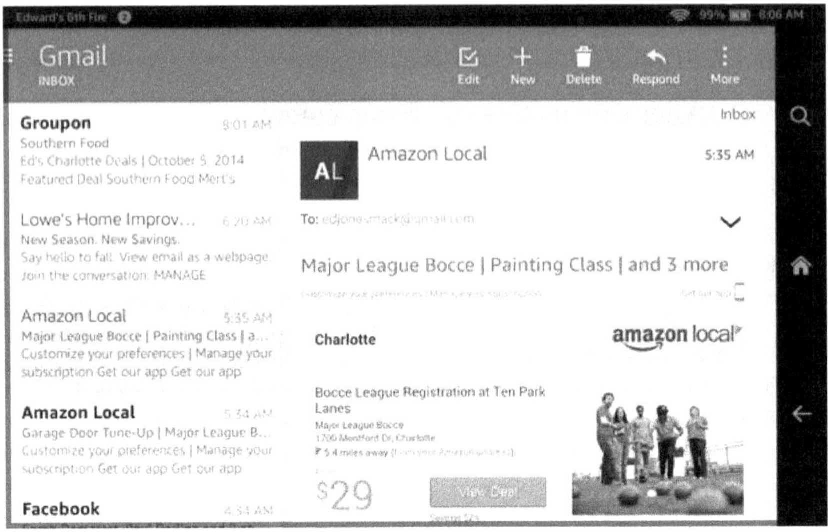

To read an e-mail, just open the Inbox, and tap the desired mail item in the list at the left to open the mail. When you do so, its content will appear in the active portion of the screen, at the right.

Switching between multiple mail accounts

If you've set up more than one e-mail account, you can switch by tapping the Menu icon (at the top left corner of the E-mail screen). An e-mail sidebar will open, and you can tap the inbox name for the account you want to check.

The Fire HD6 e-mail app has a nice feature called the ***combined inbox***, which displays mail from multiple accounts simultaneously (assuming that you have set up more than one e-mail account on your device). Tap the Menu icon (at the top left corner of the E-mail screen), and choose Combined Inbox from the sidebar that opens. Once you do this, you will see all messages from all established accounts within a single list.

Composing and Sending Mail

Writing email is also a straightforward process. At the Home screen tap Apps, then tap the E-Mail icon to get into the e-mail app. When your Inbox opens, note the toolbar that appears at the upper right, as shown in the following illustration. Using the toolbar buttons, you can compose a new e-mail, reply to an e-mail, or delete an e-mail from your Inbox.

Once in the e-mail app, tap the New icon in the toolbar to display a New Message screen, and enter the recipient's e-mail address in the To box. (Alternately, you can tap the Contacts icon and choose an address that's in your Contacts list.) When entering multiple names, separate any additional names with commas. (You can also use the Cc: and Bcc: fields to add copied recipients and blind copied recipients, respectively.)

In the Subject area, enter a subject for the message, and then enter the desired message text in the Message area. You can add attachments (such as photos stored on your Fire HD6) by tapping the icon of a paper clip at the right side of the message. When you tap this icon, the menu shown here opens, and you can choose Attach a Photo, Attach File, or Capture a Photo from the menu. (If you choose Attach a Photo, you can select an image stored in the \Pictures folder of your Fire HD6, while choosing Attach File lets you select a file that is stored in your \Documents folder of your Fire HD6. Choose Capture a Photo to take a photo using one of the built-in cameras of the Fire HD6, and immediately send that photo as an attachment.

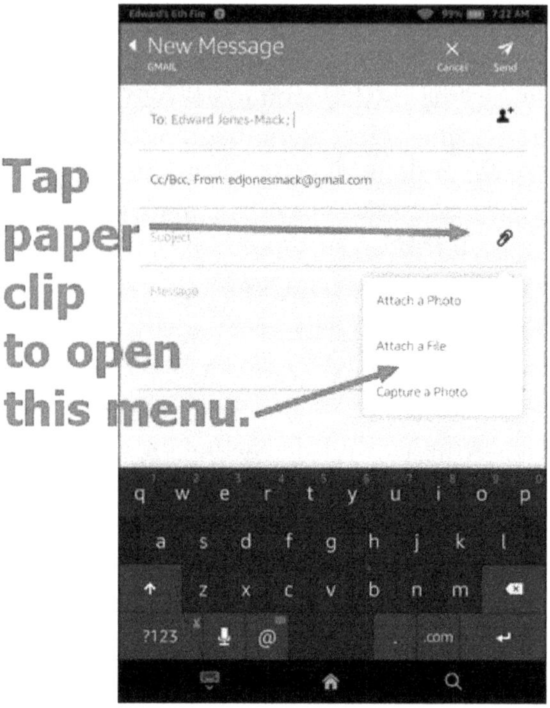

When done composing your message and adding any necessary attachments, tap the Send icon in the upper-right portion of the toolbar to send your message.

Customize your E-mail operation with various settings

Speed up your email performance by hiding images. If you receive a large amount of email that contains embedded images, display of your messages can be slowed by the presence of the images. You can turn off the display of embedded images by default. Pull down the Navigation bar, tap Settings, and under Applications, within the 'Amazon Applications' subcategory, tap 'Email, Contacts,

Calendar. At the next screen that appears, tap Email Settings. You will a screen similar to the following:

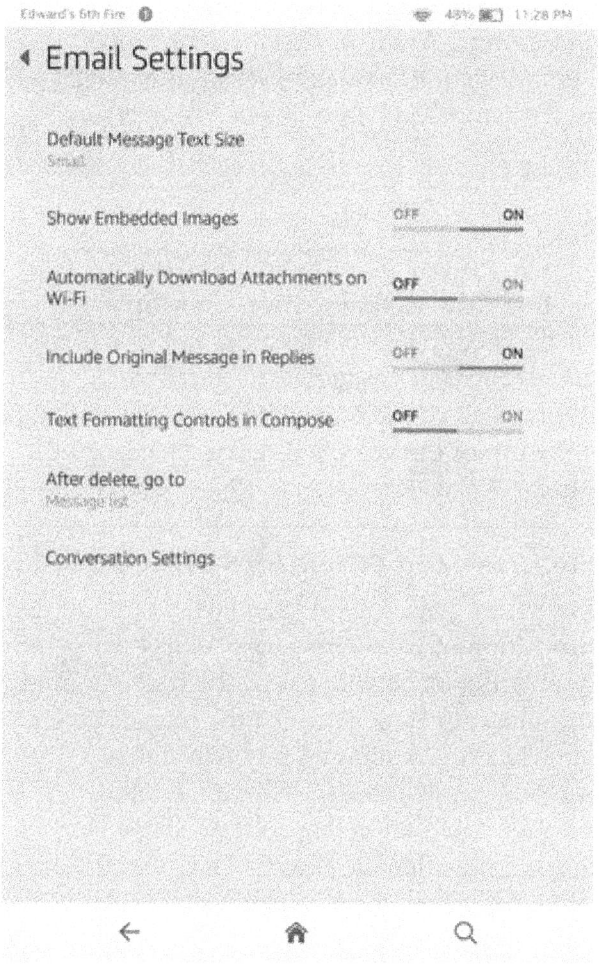

Show embedded images is normally on by default at this screen. Set this option to Off to speed up your mail performance.

Add a custom signature to save typing time. You can add a default signature line to the bottom of your outgoing messages, to save yourself the time involved in having to sign every letter that you compose. To do this, drag down the Navigation bar and tap Settings, then at the Settings screen, tap Applications, then tap Email/Contacts/Calendar, and then tap Email Settings. At the next screen that appears select the desired email account by name, scroll down within the dialog box, tap Signature, and enter the desired personal signature.

Use Bulk delete to delete multiple messages. There is no need to delete messages one at a time if you want to delete a group of messages. Just turn on the checkboxes at the left of all of the unwanted messages, and tap the Delete icon at the top of the screen to delete the selected messages as a group.

Using your synchronized calendars and contacts

Once you've set up your e-mail accounts, assuming that you allow synchronization of calendars and contacts with your e-mail accounts, you will also be able to use the Calendar and Contacts apps built into your Fire HD6. At the Home screen, tap Apps, then tap Calendar. A view of a synchronized calendar from your Google, Microsoft, iCloud, or Yahoo account will appear (the illustration that follows shows an example of a synchronized calendar based on a Google account).

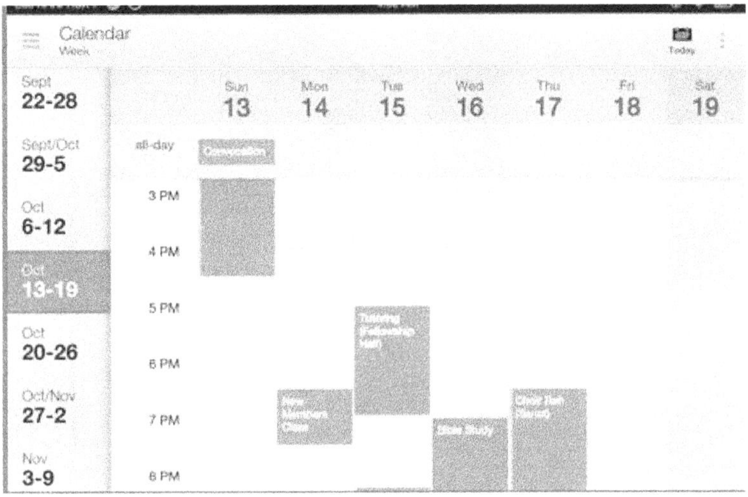

You can make changes or additions to your calendar by tapping within any date and time field, and then tapping the Plus (+) symbol that appears. A New Event screen will appear, and you can enter the details about your calendar event.

To see your synchronized contacts list, get to the Home screen, tap Apps, and locate and tap the Contacts icon. A synchronized contacts list will appear; the following illustration shows an example of a Contacts list based on a Google account. (And yes, the author does have a fondness for dead presidents, particularly the ones depicted on greenbacks, but that is another story.)

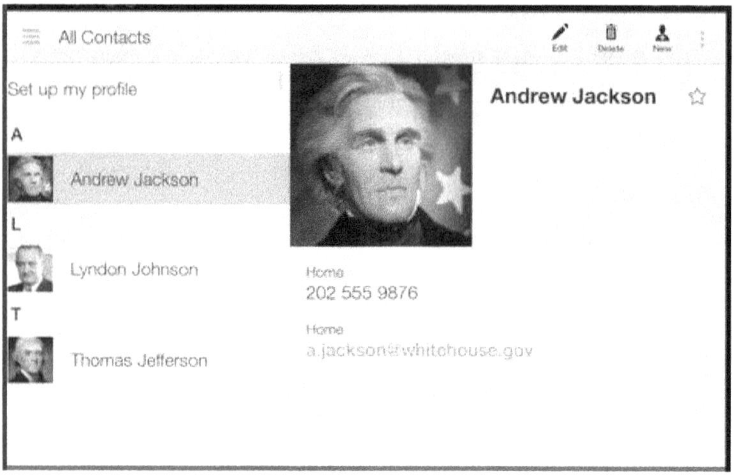

When viewing any contact, you can use the toolbar buttons that appear at the upper-right to edit an existing contact in your list, to delete a contact, or to add a new contact. As with the calendar, since the accounts are synchronized with those of your e-mail provider, any changes that you make using your Fire HD6 will be entered in the cloud-based contacts list provided by your e-mail provider.

Chapter 8: Multimedia Tips, Tricks, and Traps

One of the major strengths of the Fire centers on its impressive multimedia capabilities. Designed to provide you with a better multimedia experience, the Fire HD6 is small enough to hold in your hand, yet delivers a vibrant viewing experience with over 16 million colors on its high definition screen. The sharp, beautiful color display is backed by a speaker for audio playback built into the device, along with a headphone jack. For the technically inclined, the Fire HD6 supports 3gp and mp4 video formats, H264 video encoding, with an 800 by 480 resolution and a 2500 kps bit rate. On the audio side, the Fire HD6 supports Dolby noise reduction, AAC, MP3, MIDI, OGG, and WAV formats, and uses AAC for audio encoding of movies' audio tracks.

Playing personal videos on your Fire HD6

Play your personal videos on your Fire. You can transfer video files or download video files and play them on your Fire. You cannot place them in the video library, but you can copy your personal videos into the /Pictures subfolder of your Fire HD6 (and no, "/Pictures" is not a misprint). Your videos will appear alongside your photos when you tap Photos on the Navigation bar. The only visual difference between your photos and your videos will be the presence of an arrow within a circle, like this:

which acts as a "Play" button for the video player. Tap the arrow, and your video will begin playing on your Fire HD6's screen.

You can copy files that are stored in the 3GP or MP4 video format into the /Pictures folder that appears in the directory of folders shown on your computer when the Fire is connected by means of the USB cable. When you connect the Fire to the micro USB side of the charging cable and connect the standard USB side of the cable to your computers USB port, the Fire appears on your computer's File Explorer or file management system as a USB flash drive, similar to the example shown in the following illustration.

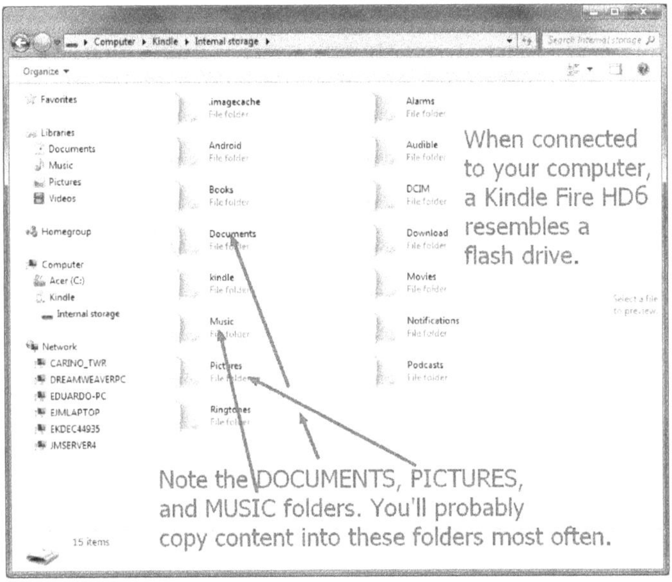

You can then use standard cut / copy / paste or drag-and-drop procedures to copy the video file from the source folder that contains the video file on your hard drive to the destination folder that appears with all the other folders of your Fire's internal storage under the device name 'Fire.'

You can copy your photos, images, or personal video files into the /Pictures folder, and these will appear within a tiled directory style view when you tap Photos in the

Navigation bar on your Home screen. In a similar fashion, you can copy .mp3 files into the /Music subfolder, and these will appear as songs when you tap Music in the Navigation bar. You can copy Microsoft Word documents, rich text format (,RTF) files, and text (.TXT) files into the /Documents folder, and these will appear when you tap Documents in the Navigation bar.

A file may exist in the acceptable file format of 3GP or MP4, yet may refuse to play on a Fire. Not only must the files be stored as a 3GP or MP4 format, the length by width (800 by 480) and video bitrate (2500) must fall within acceptable parameters, or the video will fail to play. You can use a conversion program on a desktop or laptop computer to convert video files such as your vacation movies shot with a DV camcorder to a format that will play on your Fire.

There is an excellent free, open source program for converting video files to the Fire format, and the program is available for the Windows PC, Apple Mac, and Ubuntu Linux machines. The program, Miro, can be downloaded at http://www.getmiro.com. The program may appear slightly complicated to use, at least initially. Fortunately, the getmiro.com website provides extensive documentation.

Importing your Music Library from other sources to your Fire HD6

Import your iTunes, Microsoft Zune, or other music library into your Fire using the Amazon Cloud Player. Amazon has an easy to use tool that makes importing your iTunes of other music library a simple matter. Open a browser window on your computer, and visit http://www.amazon.com/cloudplayer (if you are in North America) or visit http://www.amazon.co.uk/cloudplayer (if you are in the United Kingdom) and set up a CloudPlayer account. Once you set up an account, click the Import Music button at the upper left, and follow the directions that appear on the screen. After you've imported your songs into the Amazon Cloud Player, you can select any number of songs, click the download button, and download them to your Fire.

Downloading and playing YouTube videos

Download YouTube videos for later playback on your Fire. YouTube has long supported the H.264 video encoding format that is currently used by the Fire. And if a subject has ever been recorded on video, chances are that it can be found on YouTube, at least in partial, if not in complete form. YouTube is known for being the resource for millions of video clips. You don't even have to resort to using a PC or a Mac to download YouTube videos, because numerous YouTube video downloader apps are available for the Fire. A search of the Amazon app store for the phrase 'youtube downloader' will reveal a number of entries. One that has been tested by this author is the Droid Youtube Downloader by KastorSoft. The app is simple to use, it does what is expected of it, and it is free. (The app is ad supported, but the ads are small and fairly unobtrusive.)

Install the app, and its operation is simplicity itself. You launch the app, and a search box appears at the top of the screen. Type a search term, tap the magnifying glass, and the app will search the entire YouTube database for videos that match your search term. Find a desired video and tap the video, and another menu appears. From this menu, you can choose to preview the video, download the file as video, download the file as an MP3 audio file, or download the file as an AAC video file. Select Download as Video, and you will see a message indicating the percentage of progress saved, then a message indicating when the download is complete.

Once the YouTube video has completed downloading, go to your Apps screen and bring up your Personal Videos app. You will see an icon displaying the starting screen of the YouTube video, and you can tap the icon to play the video.

Storing pictures and personal videos in the Amazon cloud drive

Under the heading of 'Where's My Data?, chapter 1 introduced the concept of cloud based storage, which greatly increases your possible maximum storage space by saving data to web servers that reside on the Internet. As far as multimedia goes, you can store your photos and personal videos in the cloud, on Amazon's cloud drive, to be specific. If you tap the Photos option on the Navigation bar and you never set up a cloud drive account at Amazon, you'll see a welcome screen like the following:

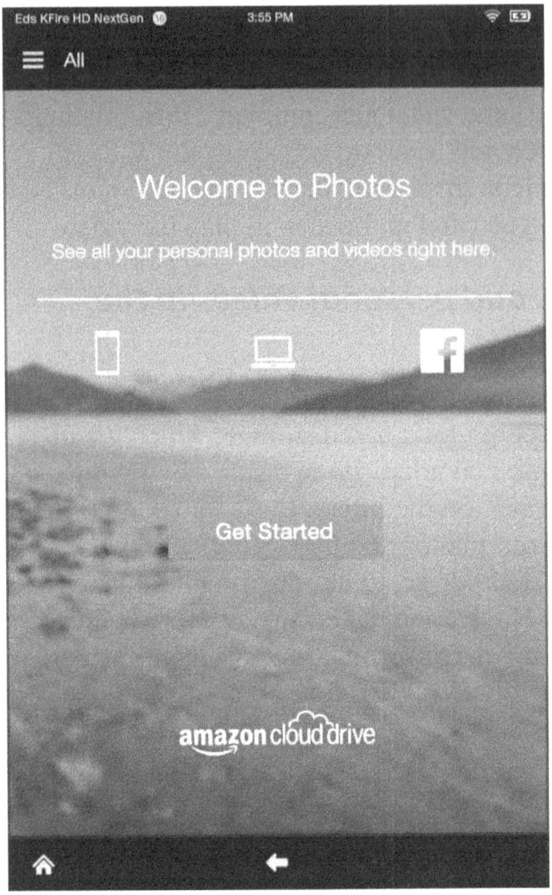

Click the Get Started link, and you will first be asked if you wish to send an app to your smartphone. (The app lets you view photos or videos stored in the Amazon cloud on your smartphone, or upload photos or videos from your phone to the Amazon cloud.) Confirm if you wish by clicking Yes and by entering your cell phone number where prompted.

Next, you will be asked if you want a link for the cloud drive app sent to your PC. Click Yes if desired, and you will receive a link via e-mail that lets you download the Amazon cloud drive app for your Windows or Apple IOS-based PC.

Once you've installed the app on a compatible smartphone or personal computer, you can move photos from your phone or your PC to Amazon's cloud drive storage.

Viewing your cloud drive photos on a Fire

After you've set up your cloud drive account and uploaded any photos, just tap Photos in the Navigation bar on your Fire HD6. Your photos will appear in a tiled based layout like that shown in the following illustration:

You can tap on any photo and it expands to fill your Fire HD6's screen, like the example shown:

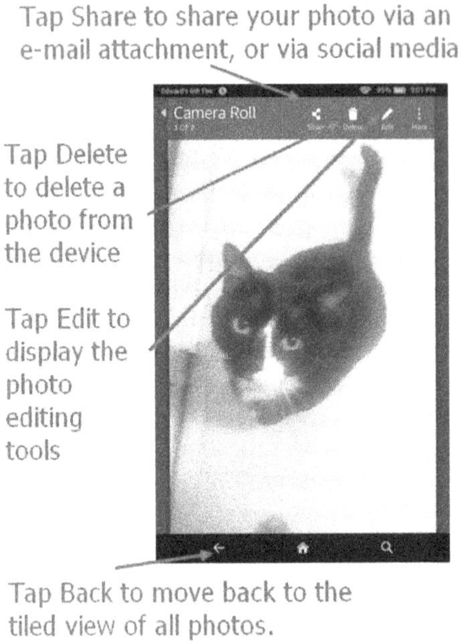

You can also perform a long press (press and hold) on any photo in your collection, and a popup menu will appear. Your menu choices are Share, Edit, Info, Download, and Delete.

Share lets you share the photo, either by means of an e-mail account, or through Facebook or Twitter, if these are linked to your Fire HD6 by means of the social settings.

Edit launches the native Photo Editor that you can use to make changes to your photos. You can change the brightness or contrast, crop your photo, reduce red eye, apply filters, and apply other special effects.

Print sends the photo to a wireless printer that may be linked to your Fire HD6.

Info displays digital information stored about the photo, including the filename, creation date, dimensions (in pixels), and file size.

Download downloads the photo onto your device from the Amazon cloud, so that you will not need a Wi-Fi connection to display the photo.

Delete deletes the photo from your device.

The Amazon Cloud Storage account provides you with 5 GB of storage space, which is roughly enough to store over 2200 average photos. This amount of storage space would easily consume most of what is available on a Fire HD6 purchased with the standard 8 GB of memory. Since the Amazon cloud drive account costs you nothing with a 5 GB allotment, it is well worth your taking the time to install and use the Amazon cloud drive app.

Mirroring your Kindle Fire to your Big-Screen TV

You can "mirror" all more recent models of Kindle Fire tablets to many TV sets, including most smart" TVs, any streaming device using the Miracast standard, and any TV equipped with Amazon Fire TV or Amazon Fire TV Stick. Mirroring takes any display that you see on a Fire tablet, along with any audio, and reproduces it at your TV. The Fire tablet must be a model produced after September 2012 (a "3rd generation" or "4th generation" model).

Before you mirror the screen of your Fire tablet, ensure your TV or media streaming device is turned on and "discoverable," meaning that your Fire tablet can locate and connect to your device using your Wi-Fi network. With Amazon Fire TV or Fire TV Stick, scroll down the main menu of Fire TV and select the 'Settings' option, then choose 'Display and Sounds,' and at the next screen select 'Enable Display Mirroring.' With "smart" TVs or TVs equipped with Miracast streaming devices, refer to the user guide for your TV or streaming device for the exact steps needed to make your device "discoverable."

Once your hardware (on the "TV" side of the equation) is ready, you can mirror your Fire display with these steps:

1. Swipe down from the top of the screen of your Fire to open Quick Settings.
2. Tap Settings.
3. Tap Display and Sounds.
4. Tap Display Mirroring. Your Fire tablet will now display all compatible devices within wireless range.
5. Find your TV or streaming device within the list and tap the device name to connect.

Note that the initial connection may take as long as 30 seconds. If your Fire tablet is able to mirror the display and audio on the other device, you'll see "Mirroring" beneath your device name. You can tap Stop Mirroring to stop mirroring the screen of your Fire.

TIP: In the author's experience, mirroring can be finicky. On at least two occasions, I've been unable to successfully connect, and both devices were Amazon products (a Fire HDX 8.9 and both a Fire TV console and a Fire TV Stick). If you are unable to mirror on the first attempt, try rebooting both your Fire tablet and the streaming device or smart TV. (If you are using Fire TV or Fire TV Stick, unplug the power cord from the Fire TV device, turn the TV off and on, and re-connect power to the Fire TV console or stick.) After rebooting both devices, you will again need to make your smart TV or streaming device "discoverable."

Chapter 9: Camera Tips, Tricks, and Traps

One of the many features found in the Fire HD6 that you generally won't find in under-$100 Android tablets is the inclusion of two digital cameras. The Fire HD6 sports both a front-facing VGA digital camera, and a rear facing 2 megapixel camera that supports 720 pixel video.

The cameras can be used to take pictures with the built-in Camera app, or with a number of 3rd-party applications available from the Amazon Appstore. You can use the cameras for video chat with the Skype app, available as a free download from the Amazon AppStore. You can also use the Facebook app to take and share photos with Facebook friends.

When viewing the Fire HD6 with its volume buttons facing to the upper right, the front-facing camera is located within the small circle at the right center of the device, as shown in the first illustration that follows. The rear-facing camera is located within the small circle at the lower right corner of the device, as shown in the second illustration that follows.

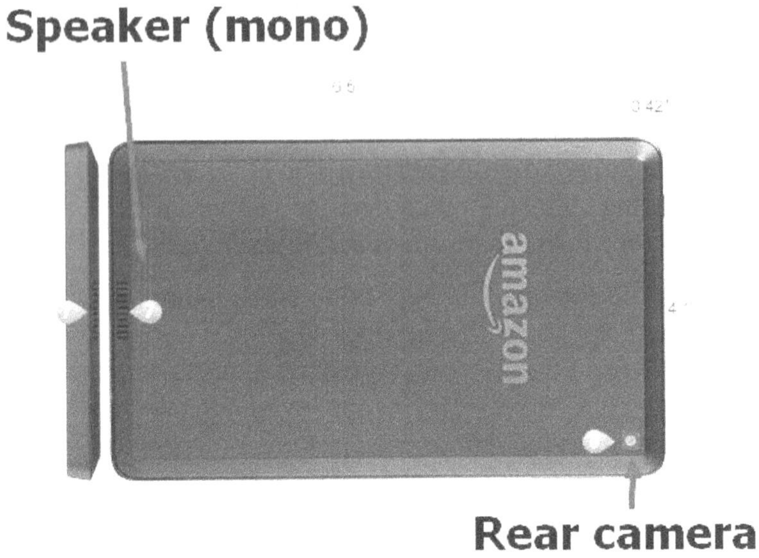

The front-facing camera is a VGA-resolution camera, and there is no flash included, so don't expect great results under low lighting. The rear-facing camera is a 2.0 megapixel camera that supports 720-pixel resolution (not true high definition but certainly better than standard VGA). The cameras perform adequately under average lighting conditions, and if you are using a camera app, you'll gain access to a number of user adjustable features that can enhance the quality of photos or videos. Since the front facing camera is facing towards you as you view the screen, it's clear that Amazon designed it initially to support video chatting or video conferencing with apps such as the Skype app. But since the release of the second-generation Fire line, the built-in Camera app has undergone a number of improvements, that let you do much more with the built-in cameras than just video chat, and take simple portraits, and that is the subject of this chapter.

Using the Fire HD6's built-in Camera app

Take photos or videos with the built-in camera app. A basic camera app comes built into the Fire HD6 software, and it does a perfectly acceptable job of taking basic pictures or videos. Before taking any photos or videos with the camera, you should take the time to ensure that the camera lens is clean and free of any dust or other obstructions. Once you've done so, get to the Home screen, tap Apps, and locate and tap the Camera icon to open the Camera app. The following illustration shows the screen and the controls that are visible when you use the Camera App.

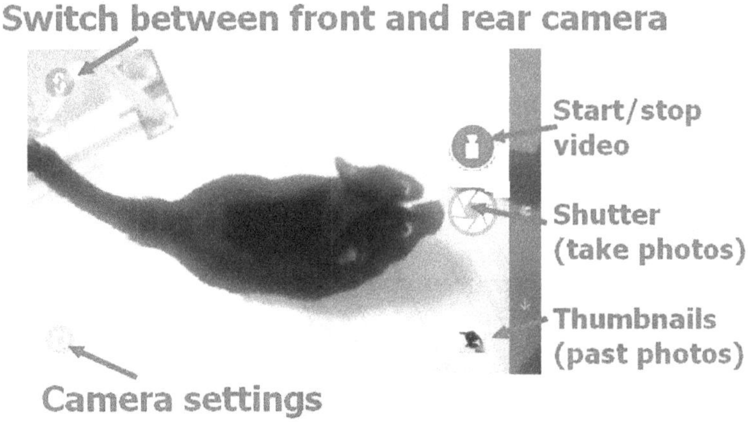

(Fire HD6 camera controls)

Tap the Shutter control to take photos in Camera mode, or tap the Start/Stop Video control to begin or end video recording.

With video recording, you can pinch the screen with two fingers to zoom in, or spread two fingers apart on the screen to zoom outwards. Once recording begins, tapping the Start/Stop Video control again will stop the video recording.

With the rear camera, use the Volume buttons as a zoom control. The rear-facing camera has a Zoom feature that is activated through the use of the volume buttons on the Fire HD6. By default, the camera starts at 1X magnification. Pressing the volume-up button increases the magnification to a maximum of 2X (twice normal size), and once increased, pressing the volume-down button decreases the magnification.

Viewing photos with the Camera Roll

After you've taken a photo or recorded a video, you can tap the thumbnail to see your Camera Roll, which enables you to view your most recent photos or videos. You can swipe to the left or to the right to move through the photos and videos contained in your Camera Roll.

To edit, delete, or view details (such as the creation date and time of your photos or videos), tap the Menu icon, shown here.

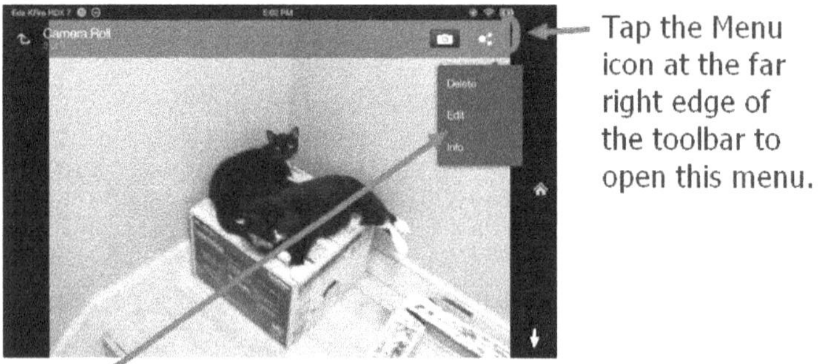

Choose Print to send a photo to a compatible printer; Info to see the creation date and time and dimensions; or Download to download the photo to your Downloads folder.

The menu provides you with three choices: Print, Info, and Download. Choose Print to print to a compatible wireless printer (see chapter 12 for more details about printing from your Fire HD6). Info displays a dialog box containing information about the photo, including the date and time created, the filename, its dimensions, and the amount of memory space used by the photo. The Download option copies the photo into your Downloads directory, where it can be accessed by many other apps. (You can also use the techniques covered earlier in Chapter 6 to copy the photo from your Downloads directory to your computer.)

Editing and Deleting Photos

When any single photo is visible on the Camera Roll, the toolbar at the top of the screen shows icons labelled 'Share', 'Edit', and 'Delete', in addition to the Menu icon. The Delete choice deletes the current photo from your device.

Tapping Edit brings up a built-in photo editor which lets you apply a variety of effects to your photo, such as changing the brightness or contrast, modifying exposure levels and eliminating 'redeye,' cropping, and adding text or drawings to a photo. While viewing any photo, tap the photo to display the toolbar at the top of the screen, and then tap the Edit icon to launch the Photo Editor. When the Photo Editor starts, you will see a menu at the bottom of the screen that displays a variety of photo editing categories, as shown in the following illustration.

Tap any category to view the editing tools for that category. If there is just one tool in a category, you will be taken to that tool. If there are multiple tools for a category, simply tap a desired tool to use it.

When you are finished editing the photo, tap Apply to save your edits. (If you decide not to use a chosen photo editing tool, swipe up from the bottom of the screen to return to the Photo Editor categories.)

When you are finished using the Photo Editor, tap Done at the upper right to exit from the app.

Sharing your photos with others

While you are displaying any photo or video in the Camera Roll, you can tap the Share icon in the toolbar area, to bring up a menu of sharing options that you can use to share photos or videos with friends. The Share icon is shown here:

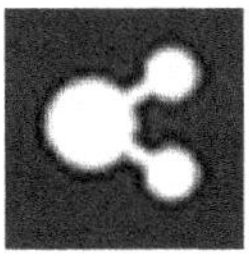

Tap the icon, and a menu of choices that include Twitter, Facebook, and e-mail appears. (Additional choices may appear on this menu, depending on the apps that you have installed on your device.) You can select any of those choices to share your photos or videos by means of the Twitter or Facebook social networks, by means of an e-mail attachment, or by means of another app on your device that has photo-sharing capabilities, such as Pinterest or Instagram.

An important note about photo & video storage and the Amazon Cloud Drive

By default, all photos and videos that you take using the built-in cameras of any Kindle Fire are backed up to your Amazon Cloud Drive account. If you do not want this copying of your files to the Amazon Cloud Drive to occur, drag the menu outwards from the left edge of the screen, tap Settings, and then turn the **Automatic Updates** option to **Off**.

Getting photos from your Fire HD6 onto your computer

You can copy photos from your Fire directly to your computer. One way to move photos from your Fire to your computer is to send the photos by e-mail, but there's another method that is often faster, especially when you have a large number of photos. You can transfer photos from your Fire to your computer using the following steps. First, connect the Fire to the computer using the USB cable. Open the Computer folder on your computer. (If you are running

Windows, you can go to the Start menu and select Computer.) Open the Computer folder and select Fire, then open that folder and select the Internal Storage folder. Open the Internal Storage folder and look for a folder named DCIM.

Open the DCIM folder and look for a folder named Camera. Open the Camera folder, and you will see your photos taken with the camera. Select the photos that you want to transfer to your computer, then right click and select Cut from the menu that appears if you want to move the photos from your Fire, or select Copy from the menu that appears if you want to keep a copy of the photos on your Fire. Finally, navigate to the folder on your computer where you want to place your photos, then right click and select Paste.

If you can't find your photos, try a reset. At times, the Kindle's MediaScanner service does not see new pictures immediately. In order for photos and videos to show up, they have to be scanned and indexed by the MediaScanner service that is a part of the operating system running on the Fire HD6. If you wait long enough, they will eventually show up, but you can force them to appear by simply restarting your Fire HD6.

You can quickly delete unwanted photos while viewing them. When any photo is visible, perform a long-press near the center of the photo. When a popup menu appears, tap "Delete" to delete the photo.

Adding capabilities with optional third-party camera apps

Use an Optional Camera App with the Fire HD6 for more capabilities. If you plan to make any extensive use of the Fire HD6's built in cameras, you may want to download a camera app for your machine. While the built-in camera app provides a variety of editing capabilities, a number of third-party camera apps provide additional capabilities, such as increased zoom, special effects, delay timers, and the ability to pause and resume video recordings. A search of the Amazon AppStore for the phrase 'camera app' will reveal an assortment of dozens of apps. (When shopping for a camera app—or for any 3rd-party app for that matter—examining the customer reviews is a wise idea, as the quality of 3rd-party apps in general ranges from outstanding to mediocre at best.)

General Camera tips, tricks, and traps

If you make use of an optional camera app purchased from the AppStore and your camera app has a 1080 pixel setting, do NOT try to use it with the front-facing camera! Some third-party camera apps have a 1080 pixel setting within their video settings. This setting exists because these apps are written to run on other Android devices, many of which are based on hardware supporting the 1080 pixel resolution (such as the Fire HDX 8.9-inch model with rear-facing high-definition camera). The front-facing camera on any Fire does ***not*** support this resolution, and if you select such an option, the app will probably crash and you may have to restart your Fire. (While the Fire HD6's display may qualify as high-definition, the front-facing camera does not.) If

the app that you are using has an option for resolution settings, avoid any settings higher than 720 pixels.

When filming video, you may need to turn the camera "upside down." If you are using an optional third-party camera app that supports video filming, you may discover that the Fire HD6 gives proper results when the built-in camera is facing downwards, and not at the top of the device. (This behavior doesn't appear to affect all apps that support video, but it does appear to affect some third-party apps, so you may want to check the operation of your chosen app before attempting to record that all-important wedding or graduation using your Fire HD6.)

Chapter 10: Apps Tips, Tricks, and Traps

In this chapter, we look at the power of apps to add significant features and capabilities to your Fire. The tablet would be impressive if it were only used for reading books and magazines, for watching movies and TV shows, and for web browsing. But with a range of apps available from the Amazon AppStore, you can transform your Fire in an unlimited number of ways. Using apps, you can literally transform your Fire into a news or weather information center, a sports scoreboard, an international language translator, a customized radio station, a medical adviser, or a personal butler that reminds you of every appointment on your busy daily schedule. And of course, you can use an app to make your Fire into a game platform, so that you can play a few rounds of Angry Birds. This chapter will first detail various tips, tricks, and traps for apps in general, in a section we like to call 'Apps 101.' We will follow that with a listing of twenty apps that we feel that no Fire should be without.

About Apps

Apps for your Fire (or for any tablet computer, for that matter) are actually computer programs, engineered to handle a specific task. As such, they must be ***installed*** on your Fire, which is a sophisticated computer in its own right. You can obtain apps on your Fire by first purchasing the app (even if it's free) from the Amazon AppStore. You then install the app on your Fire by pressing the 'Download' button that appears once you purchase the app. After the app has been installed on your Fire, the download button changes to display the word 'Open', and you can press the Open button to start the app. Once the app exists on your Fire, you can get to it at any time, by choosing Apps from the Home screen, and locating and pressing on the icon for the particular app.

Find and install the app you want. At the Home screen, tap Apps, then at the upper right, tap Store. When the main screen of the Amazon AppStore appears, tap in the Search AppStore box at the top of the screen. The box will expand, and the keyboard will appear within the lower portion of the screen. Enter a search term to bring up one or more apps matching your search term, then tap the icon for the app that you are looking for.

Can I run generic android apps that don't come from the Amazon AppStore?

The short answer to the above question is an unqualified "maybe," but it's also a topic that is far beyond the scope of this book. You may be aware of the fact that your Fire runs a modified version of the popular Android operating system originally developed by Google. And you may be aware of the existence of android apps from other sources on the web (such as Google's own Play Store). While it is possible to run some of these apps on a Fire, it takes some tinkering with settings, and it's not a practice that Amazon recommends. Nevertheless, if you are interested in pursuing this topic further, you are definitely moving into "geek" territory. As an accomplished geek, my recommendation is that (1) you tread very carefully when journeying into this area and (2) you refer to a "geek" level treatment of the topic. You can perform a Google search on the phrase, 'how to install playstore on the Fire,' and a number of articles will appear in response to the search. Some will be well-written, and others will make you regret having ever asked the question to begin with.

Deleting Apps

There will be times you'll want to delete an app, perhaps because it's not what you expected, or it is a game you've outgrown, or something better comes along. Apps are stored in two places: in your cloud storage on Amazon's servers, and on your Fire itself. When you initially purchase an app (even free apps are purchased, you just aren't charged for these), the app is stored in your personal space in the Amazon Cloud, where the app is not taking up any space on your Fire. When you press the download button that appears on the apps' icon in the cloud, it gets downloaded to the memory space of your Fire itself.

Remove unwanted apps from your Fire. You can remove any app from the Fire by displaying all of your apps (tap “Apps” in the Navigation menu), then performing a "long press" on the apps icon, and choosing 'Remove from Device' from the popup menu that appears. The long press simply means that you press and hold your finger on the icon for a few seconds, until a check box appears over the icon. At the Home screen, press Apps to display your apps screen. When the apps screen appears, select 'Device' near the top center of the screen, to display all the apps currently stored on your Fire.

Press and hold your finger on the icon of the unwanted app until a menu appears, then select 'Remove from Device' from the menu. This action will delete the app from your Kindle's memory space.

An app that’s deleted from your Fire can still be taking up space in your cloud. Keep in mind that deleting an app from your Fire itself does not remove the app from your storage in the Amazon Cloud. If you want to delete the app from cloud storage as well, go to your Home screen, tap Apps, and then tap 'Cloud' near the top center of the screen.

This will reveal all your apps that are stored in the Amazon Cloud.

Locate the unwanted app, and press and hold your finger on the app icon until a popup menu appears, then choose 'Remove from Cloud' from the menu. ***Note that deleting an app from your cloud storage at Amazon also wipes away any subscription information you may have saved in the app, so you should do this only if you are certain that you do not want to use the app in the future.***

Troubleshooting Apps

As mentioned earlier, apps are computer programs. And like all computer programs, they will at times fail to operate as promised, misbehave, or go absolutely haywire. When an app fails to operate as expected, your steps in resolving the issue will vary greatly depending on what type of behavior the app exhibited in the first place. Some app failures fall into the 'hiccup' category, in which case it may be best to chalk it up to the "evil gods of operating systems" and to move on in life. Other failures can go beyond the level of major annoyance; as an example, a camera app for my Fire recently caused my Fire's sound to stop working in all applications, and the only fix was to perform a hard reboot and completely reset my Fire to factory settings. If an app misbehaves, crashes, or completely locks up your Fire, here are some procedures that you can try, ranging in ascending order from minor (meaning, 'let's hope this works') to major (meaning, 'lets hope you don't have to resort to this')-

1. ***Close and restart the app.*** Without subjecting you to a heavy dose of techno-babble, let's just say that Android-based computers tend to be more stable than some small computer operating systems (Windows, not that anyone is pointing fingers) because each Android app runs in something called ***protected space***. From a programming point of view, each app can "play inside its own sandbox." This means that in theory, the abnormal operation of an app should not affect the

entire operating system, nor should it have an effect on other apps. When an app misbehaves, the least troublesome step is to completely close the app, then restart the app. If this does not fix the problem you can move on to-

2. ***Perform a soft reset on your Fire.*** This happens naturally whenever you power down the machine, so just try turning it off. Wait 10 seconds, and power the Fire back on, then try the app again. If the soft reset fails to bring your machine back to normal operation, you can resort to-

3. ***Perform a hard reset.*** With the Kindle powered up, press and hold the power button depressed until you see a "Power off?" prompt appear on the screen. Tap 'Yes' in response to this prompt, and your Kindle will shut down. Wait 10 seconds, and power your Kindle back up. You may notice a distinct difference in the appearance of the startup sequence this time, as the ‘Amazon’ logo in white will appear in the center of the screen followed by the word ‘fire’ in orange. This simple display will remain for a short period of time (less than 2 minutes) while the machine restarts. Hopefully, this will fix the issue, because the most drastic step will also result in a definite loss of settings. But if you must resort to the most drastic step--

4. ***Reset your Fire to its default directory settings***. Be warned that if use this last resort, you will need to reset your username and e-mail account information that you've registered with Amazon into the device, and you will have to pull all your apps back down from the Amazon cloud (and reenter any user settings that may have been stored in these apps). To perform this ultimate reboot, use the following steps:

a. At the Home screen, tap and drag down from the top of the screen, and tap Settings.

b. At the next screen, choose 'Device.'

c. At the next screen, choose ‘Reset to Factory Defaults.’

If your Fire still has operational issues after this type of reset, it is definitely time to get on the phone with Amazon Customer Service.

Twenty FREE Apps That No Fire Should Be Without

As promised, here's a listing of 20 FREE apps (you heard correctly, the price is zero, nada, zilch) that this author believes should be on the carousel of every Fire. This is an admittedly subjective list, but each of these apps has also received a high average rating (between 4 and 5 stars) from Amazon reviewers.

Note that the write-ups of the 20 free apps that follow are excerpted from the publication, ***Top 300 (Plus) Free Apps for the Kindle Fire*** by this same author. If you would like to see the other 280-something recommendations detailed in that book, consider a visit to the Amazon store (www.amazon.com) and spending the reasonable sum of ninety-nine cents on *Top 300 (Plus) Free Apps for the Kindle Fire* by Edward Jones.

Crackle

Crackle is an outstanding source of FREE (that's correct, as in 'no subscrber or pay-per-view fees imvolved) movies and TV shows. With the Crackle app installed on yor Kindle Fire, you get immediate access to thousands of full-length Hollywood movies and TV shows. At the time this was written, the lineup on Crackle included movies like Pineapple Express, Big Daddy, Joe Dirt, Mr. Deeds, Alien Hunter, The Deep, Panic Room, S.W.A.T., and hundreds of others. Also in the Crackle lineup are dozens of TV shows like Seinfeld, The Prisoner, Marvel Comics' Iron Man animated series, All in the Family, and Chosen, just to name a few. Twenty new movies and TV episodes are added to the lineup each month, from genres that include action, anime, comedy, crime, horror, thrillers, and sci-fi. Crackle is truly free internet entertainment at its best, and unless you only purchased your Fire for reading, you shuld definitely have the Crackle app as one of your apps.

Netflix

The app may be free, but of course you'll need a Netflix subscription to actually watch any content. Given that fact, if you are a Netflix subscriber, you'll want the free Netflix app for your Fire. You can watch all of the same Netflix videos that you might see streamed to your laptop, and if you've got a Fire HD6, you can enjoy that Dolby surround sound which comes across nicely with a good pair of headphones plugged into the Kindle. Log in with your NetFlix account, and you can get their usual unlimited shows and flicks on your Fire, and can even pick up where you left off on a show you'd started watching earlier on your TV set or other portable device. Of course, no movie-viewing app would be complete without having the Internet Movie Database (IMDb) app so you can get a good idea of what you're watching before you decide to watch it; the Internet Movie Database app is described next.

IMDb

If you are a movie fan or a fan of regular TV shows, or even if you aren’t but don't want to be embarrassed by those trivia-type TV actor questions that arise when you and your friends are debating “who played in what role,” you'll want IMDb on your Fire. The app gives you access to a database of two million titles and four million cast members. It is divided into movies and TV sections, you can see what U.S. movies are getting the highest box office ratings, and you can even watch trailers for hundreds of thousands of movies. The app doesn't have anything that you couldn't get from the IMDb web site running on your laptop for desktop computer, but the interface is intuitive, the app is free, and it's easy to carry around on your Fire.

USA Today

From what multiple reviewers and this author say, the USA Today app for the Kindle Fire is the kind of app that every newspaper app should be. The content is beautiful, optimized to take advantage of the Fire's larger screen. Unlike many newspaper apps for Android-based tablets, the content is all free on this one; there are no subscription services to pay whatsoever. While you're online, the app feeds you constant updates, making sure you've received the latest news and information, and you can pull down stories for offline reading when you don't have Internet access.

The organization is logical, the formatting is colorful, and from a user friendliness standpoint it's a cinch to navigate. There is a wonderfully-intuitive 'swipe to the left or right' action within the main content viewer that automatically jumps you between stories in the smaller Articles window on the left, or you can tap any story within the Articles window to bring up the corresponding story on the right. Stories are laced with top-notch photography and occasionally with vivid video narratives. As an online newspaper, this implementation absolutely rocks. Oh, and did we mention that it's free? As a newspaper, USA Today on the Fire deserves five stars.

The Weather Channel

For the kind of in-depth weather reporting that you've come to rely on, you no longer need to turn to a cable or satellite TV channel. The Weather Channel is now no further than your Fire. Get animated and customizable radar maps; immediate, 36-hour, and ten day forecasts; severe weather alerts for the US and Europe; the ability to save multiple locations; and a "find me" feature that provides you with pinpoint local weather, based on your GPS location. Even the local pollen counts, which are often omitted from other sources, can be found at The Weather Channel. One particularly nice feature is the ability to touch a 'Video' button and get the local forecast for your area on demand from one of the TV anchors for The Weather Channel.

ESPN ScoreCenter

When it comes time to talk sports around the office water cooler on a Monday morning, you'll never be stumped for a score again if you install the ESPN ScoreCenter app on your Fire. You'll get scores, team standings, and news from hundreds of sports leagues worldwide. The variety of sports provided by ESPN ScoreCenter is just short of breathtaking- you'll find NFL and college football, NBA and college basketball, Major League Baseball, NHL Ice Hockey, and most other NCAA sports. If you are a big soccer fan, you'll find coverage of the Premier League, UEFA Champions League, the World Cup, and hundreds of additional soccer leagues and tournaments. NASCAR and Indy racing fans will find full coverage of motor sports, and golf, tennis, rugby, and cricket fans are all covered as well. If you are looking to keep up with the sports scene, you'll find it all in the ESPN ScoreCenter app.

Facebook by Facebook

This is the Facebook app for the Fire, engineered by the programmers at Facebook. It's basically the same app that was created by Facebook for generic Android-based tablets, with a few tweaks in the programming code to allow it to run under the heavily modified version of the Android operating system used by the Fire.

If you are familiar with Facebook, you have an idea of what to expect, and you do get these basics from the Facebook app. The news feed is here, and a new button at the upper right of the news feed quickly shows you who among your Facebook friends is available to message. When sending messages from within the app, you can see who is active, so you will have an idea as to when you can expect a reply. As with Facebook from the web, you can see what your friends are up to; share updates, photos, and videos; get notifications when others 'like' or comment on your posts; and text, chat, and carry on group conversations.

All that being said, the Facebook app gets a 'middle of the road' rating from Amazon reviewers, having had its fair share of teething problems. The most commonly experienced problem, according to numerous Amazon reviewers, is an inability to see more than roughly ten posts in your message wall or in the news feed. This problem has been reported to Facebook for about as long as the Facebook app has been in existence (which has been for some months now). If you install a Facebook app and you encounter the same type of behavior, you may want to uninstall the app and consider other ways to get to Facebook, one of which is mentioned in the paragraphs that follow.

Calculator Plus FREE by Digital Cherry, LLC

This app earned a listing in a “best free apps” article written by USA Today, and for good reason. Calculator Plus consistently earns five stars from reviewers, thanks to its intuitive interface, its feature set, and its ease of use. It is a simple calculator with just the basics, but those basics likely make for 98% of what most people need in a calculator. The app takes advantage of the Fire's large screen to present a very basic, but totally functional desktop style calculator. You get the basic keys (+), (-), (*), (/), and (%), along with a backspace key that works intuitively in concert with the calculator’s multiline display, allowing you to use the backspace key to “undo” past operations. This free app is ad supported, but the ads are unobtrusive and nearly impossible to accidentally hit while using the calculator function keys.

PageOnce Money and Bills by PageOnce Corp.

CNN/Money Magazine referred to this app as "the Cadillac of money management apps," and for good reason. You can use it to organize and track your basic spending, cash on hand, bills, credit cards, and the amount of money you have placed in investments. You can keep a high-level view of what you are spending, and even pay all your bills from one location (although note that to use the bill paying feature, the app has to connect with the PageOnce servers and there is a $.30 per transaction processing fee). PageOnce Money and Bills was designed to be a one-stop money-management destination. The app also helps you break down how much of your money goes toward different types of bills each month, from credit card bills to insurance bills to utilities. You will need to enter login information for your financial accounts, but the app has been certified by TRUSTe and VeriSign, so it meets high standards for mobile security.

Checkbook

by Digital Life Solutions

When you don't need all the features of a full fledged financial analysis or personal finance program, when all you want to do is balance your checkbook, there's Checkbook. This free app won't help you with money market rates nor will it make loan analysis evaluations for you, but it will do a first class job of helping you balance as many ledger accounts, checking or savings, as you wish. You can set up multiple accounts, and you can transfer amounts between accounts, and Checkbook will keep track of your running balances. You can also choose to base your account on any one of seven different currencies. You can group transactions into over 30 different transaction categories such as mortgage, rent, groceries, car payments, insurance, and so on, and you can create your own custom categories. You can also set up scheduled transactions, so that these are automatically deducted from your account. You'll find it much easier to avoid those nasty bank overdraft charges with Checkbook running on your Fire.

HotelTonight

by HotelTonight

How often have you found yourself on a trip and suddenly due to a change of plans, you need a great deal on a hotel room? Or perhaps you're partying with friends, or a drive home is taking longer than you thought and you're tired, or you're stuck late at work and just don't want to make the drive home. Whatever the reason, HotelTonight is a great app that offers last minute pricing on a variety of hotel rooms. The deals are based on the known fact that hotels often have unused rooms that they are willing to fill at the last minute for rock bottom prices. It's worth noting that's the app gets its updates on deals from its database daily at noon in whatever time zone you're searching in. So if you're looking for a great deal on a last minute hotel room, you won't see that days' deals until after 12 noon.

Kayak

by Kayak Software Corporation

Kayak is a great multi purpose travel app for your Fire that lets you search for and discover flights, hotels, and car rentals, compare prices, and even get notification of cancellations and delays and gate information for your flights. You can also access maps of restaurants and ATMs in different locations where you are travelling. If you're in need of a last minute hotel room, or worried about a gate change or a flight delayed due to weather conditions, or need a car rental or you would just like to see a map of the airport where you're making a connection, you can now do all of this in one single app, Kayak. One caveat is that the app appears to only use Hertz as a car rental source, but otherwise, this is a great app for all things travel related.

CruiseFinder

by iCruise.com

If you are a fan of cruising, this is one app that you'll want to have on your Fire. Cruise Finder is a comprehensive cruise vacation planning app that gives you extensive information concerning over 200 ships sailing with 20 different cruise lines. You'll find thousands of itineraries complete with day by day descriptions and route maps, online pricing, availability, and booking, photos of ports, stateroom descriptions and deck plans, and even parking and map information for cruise line ports. A 'Hot Cruise Deals' section keeps you up to date with last minute pricing, and a 'My Favorites' section lets you save your favorite ships, itineraries, and cruise lines.

YP Local Search and Gas Prices (Kindle tablet edition)

by YP

When your travel is more of the local variety, out and around your own hometown, the people behind the yellow pages have brought you a great little free app called YP Local Search and Gas Prices. You can search through over 16,000,000 businesses divided into major categories like restaurants, bars, hotels, doctors, dentists, mechanics, and more. You can check out the menus from over 300,000 restaurants, and you can find the gas stations that have the best gas prices in town. You can personalize your version of the app so that it is gives you fast access to nearby businesses, restaurants, and events in your town, and you can provide your own feedback by rating local businesses (you'll need to be online to enter ratings). If you live in an area of the country where gas prices can vary wildly from one neighborhood to another, this app can be worth having just for the possible savings in gas prices alone.

Adobe Reader by Adobe Systems

If you spend a fair amount of time working with documents that are in the portable document format (pdf) pioneered by Adobe, you may as well opt for the Adobe Reader as an app on your Fire. While you can open a PDF file in the default Kindle viewer, the Adobe Reader offers more features in terms of working with PDF documents. You can make the print larger or smaller at the touch of the magnification button. You can navigate in more ways, viewing documents in a single page format, or as a continuous series of pages. And you can search through a searchable pdf for a phrase, or e-mail a pdf as an attachment, things that you cannot do with the Fire's native viewer.

One feature that would have been nice to have would be a quick way to delete pdf documents from your Fire when you are done with them. That feature is sadly lacking from the Adobe Reader app for the Fire, so you will still need to manually go into your documents directory and delete unwanted files.

iTranslate by Sonico Mobile

iTranslate is a great free app that does language translation. If you're a student of languages or you do a lot of international travel, you'll definitely want to have this one on your Fire. The app does a magnificent job of combining voice recognition with voice output, so you can speak and see your language. The app will translate words, phrases, and entire sentences into any one of more than 50 languages. These words of one Amazon reviewer do a great job of describing the functionality of the program:

"I am fluent in several languages and was pretty impressed with this app. I tested with a realistic tourist phrase which was fairly complex "I would like to visit your best art museum. Can you give me a recommendation and how to get there."

I selected English from the left drop down list, typed in the phrase in English, and selected the second language from a drop down list on the right. I was impressed with the translation, the grammar was perfectly correct. Next to the text there was a button which pronounced the translation. The pronunciation was excellent and sounded like a native speaker. The intonations sounded "computer generated" but completely understandable. I tested Russian and Spanish." The reviewer goes on to state that "this was the first random sentence that came to mind, I did not try to find a phrase that would be translated well. I was quite impressed with the results."

iTranslate will even let you e-mail a translated message, share it via Twitter, or copy it into memory for use with another app. Supported languages (at the time of this writing) include the following: Afrikaans, Albanian, Arabic, Belarusian, Bulgarian, Catalan, Chinese Simplified, Chinese Traditional, Croatian, Czech, Danish, Dutch, English, Estonian, Finnish, French, Galician, German, Greek, Hebrew, Hindi, Hungarian, Icelandic, Indonesian, Italian, Irish, Japanese, Korean, Latvian, Lithuanian, Macedonian, Malay, Maltese, Norwegian, Persian, Polish, Portuguese, Romanian, Russian, Serbian, Slovak, Slovenian, Spanish, Swahili, Swedish, Tagalog, Thai, Turkish, Ukrainian, Vietnamese, Welsh, and Yiddish.

My Alarm Clock Free (by Apalon)

My Alarm Clock Free is a straightforward, flexible alarm clock app that runs nicely in the background on your Fire, until it is time to do its job and wake you from sleep. There are a variety of built-in tunes that you can use as alarms, and there is also an option that lets you fall asleep to white noise, as well as support for multiple alarms. The alarm will sound even when the app isn't running, and a built-in dimming feature changes the screen brightness, to prevent unnecessary battery drain.

Inkpad Notepad for Notes (by Workpail)

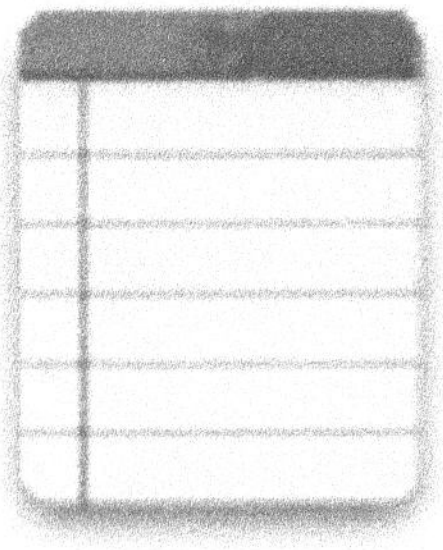

When all you need is a digital notepad, Inkpad Notepad for Notes will fill the bill. It's not designed to categorize your ideas, nor build mini-spreadsheets nor organize your friends phone numbers into small databases; it just lets you take notes. It resembles a paper notepad, and you can jot down whenever notes you like. The note is automatically saved with a title that matches the first line in the note. Tap a 'Share' button at the bottom of the note to share the note via e-mail, or by sending an SMS text message to a cell phone.

WebMD by WebMD

In these recessionary times of spiraling health care costs and many underinsured due to circumstances often beyond one's control, it's great to have an app like WebMD. WebMD is the popular online medical reference library brought to app form on the Fire. Using the symptom checker feature, you can choose the body part that is troubling you, select your symptoms, and learn about potential conditions or issues. WebMD's exhaustive drugs and treatments database gives you information on drugs, supplements, and vitamins. A First Aid Essentials guide to medical emergencies is available offline, so whether you have a wi-fi connection or not, you'll still be able to access the treatment essentials outlined in the First Aid Essentials guide.

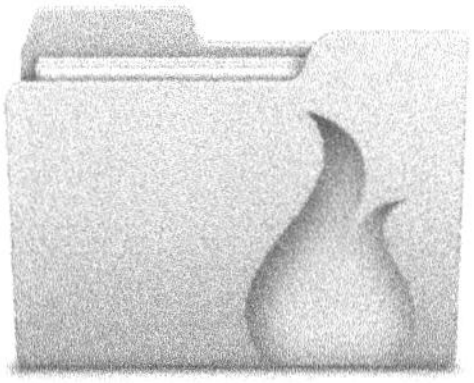

File Manager (by Appsolutely)

This great free app for the Fire lets you manage and browse files, open, delete, rename and move files, zip/unzip files, and send files via email. There are no banner ads and the app is completely free, based on the Open Source (Apache 2.0) License. A note of caution here: this app lets you see files that are normally hidden from your view on the Fire, and it's possible to wreak havoc if you don't know what you are doing.

Wi-Fi File Explorer by Dooblou

Assuming you have a home network with PCs attached to it, you don't necessarily have to resort to the annoyance of a cable connected between your Fire and your computer every time you want to move a file between the two. Wi-Fi File Explorer is a neat little app that lets you transfer files wirelessly. Download and install this free app on your Fire, and when you run the app, once you identify the wi-fi network used by the Fire, you'll see a display giving you a web address that you can point a browser on the computer that's also on your network. The address will include a port number, something similar to the following:
http://192.168.1.15:8000

Point your computer's web browser to the address you're given (yours will differ from this example) and you'll see a display like the following:

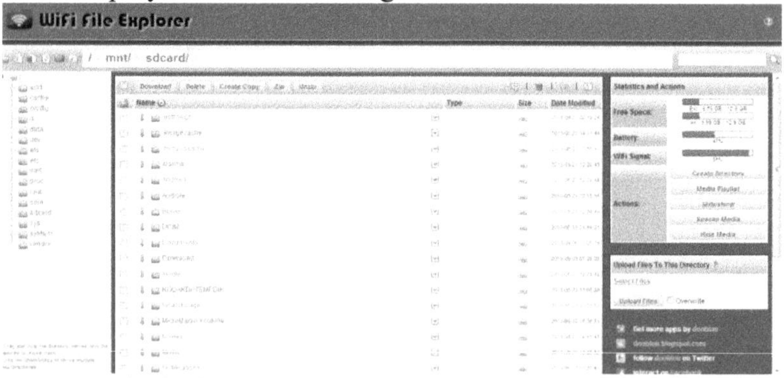

Wi-Fi File Explorer gives you a file explorer view of all the folders on your Fire HD6. You can drill down into any folder, and use the Download button at the top of the Wi-Fi File Explorer window to move files from your laptop to your Fire, without the hassle of wires.

As mentioned earlier, the write-ups of the ten free apps described in this chapter were excerpted from the publication, *Top 300 (Plus) Free Apps for the Kindle Fire* by this same author. If you would like to see the other 291 recommendations detailed in that book, consider a visit to the Amazon store for a purchase of *Top 300 (Plus) Free Apps for the Kindle Fire by Edward Jones.*

Chapter 11: Keeping Kids Safe with Parental Controls and FreeTime

There was a time when most parents worried about children losing their innocence only at the hands of older children or strangers. Sadly, those days are long passé.

Today, all it takes is the Internet.

And I'm not even referring to those "adults-only" web sites, or enticing offers from warped individuals in social chat rooms who have no business talking to minors.

A young child can see something that you, as a parent, would probably consider totally inappropriate for your child to watch after performing nothing more than a search for a favorite cartoon character on YouTube. Case in point: my own college-aged son sent me a YouTube link to a clip of the popular children's television cartoon character "Barney." In the clip, Barney, after picking flowers, was done in, in a rather horrendous graphic fashion by a character from the teen game Mortal Kombat packing an M16, armed to the teeth.

The graphic violence of that YouTube clip was not the sort of thing any parent would want their four year old to stumble upon, but if your four year old is allowed to do an unsupervised search on YouTube, it's quite possible that your four year old will run into that very same clip.

Computers in the home, since their inception, have always offered both promise and pitfalls for the development of young children. Tablets, in particular, have become an incredibly popular toy for young ones. And they can be very educational, with their phenomenal assortment of educational games and apps. You can stock a Fire with an assortment of educational games, cartoons, family oriented movies, and children's books, and these can all be used with no access to a web browser. Besides acting as an educational aid or an electronic babysitter, the Fire can be a great way to reward a child for good behavior, perhaps allowing a few rounds of a game like Angry Birds in Space.

But if you are a parent or guardian of the young child, you also know that your child isn't quite ready for many of the things that your child could see on the Internet, without going anywhere near an adult website.

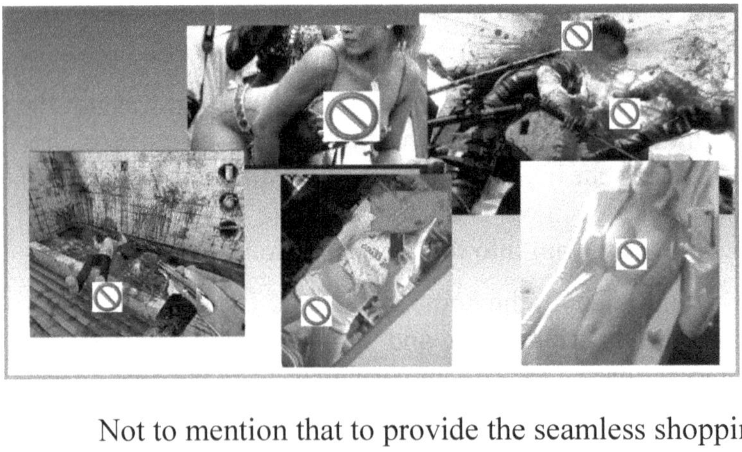

Not to mention that to provide the seamless shopping experience that the company does so well, your Fire HD6 is linked to an Amazon account with someone's credit card- presumably, yours- and you're probably not quite ready to turn that into the hands of your four year old in an unrestricted fashion, either.

Keeping Young Fire HD6 Users Off the Web

To keep your child's use of the Fire restricted to just the content that is on the Fire itself, Amazon has provided a simple-to-implement password protect option that is part of ***Parental Controls***. Drag down the Navigation bar at the top of the screen, and tap **Settings** to get to the Settings screen. Tap **Parental Controls** and change the setting from Off to **ON**, and you will see the following screen, where you will be asked to enter and reenter a password.

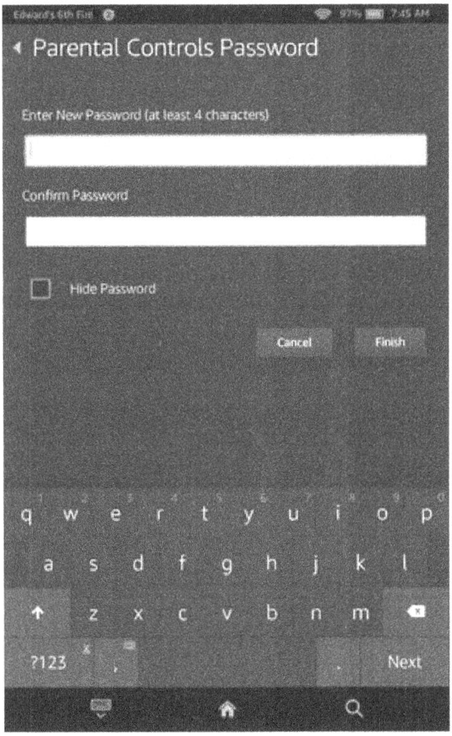

Once you enter a password, parental controls will be enabled with the default settings, as shown in the illustration here.

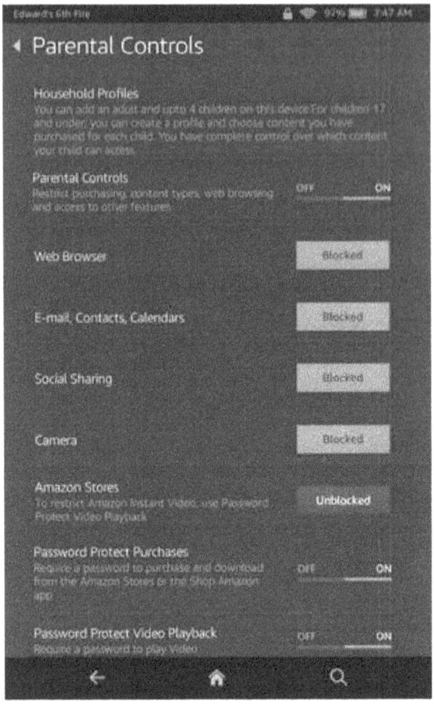

The default settings for parental controls will automatically disable access to the Silk web browser. The "Web" link in the Shortcut Bar at the top of the screen will be dimmed and unavailable. If there are any items on the Carousel or in your Favorites that are website links and you attempt to access them, you will see a message, like this:

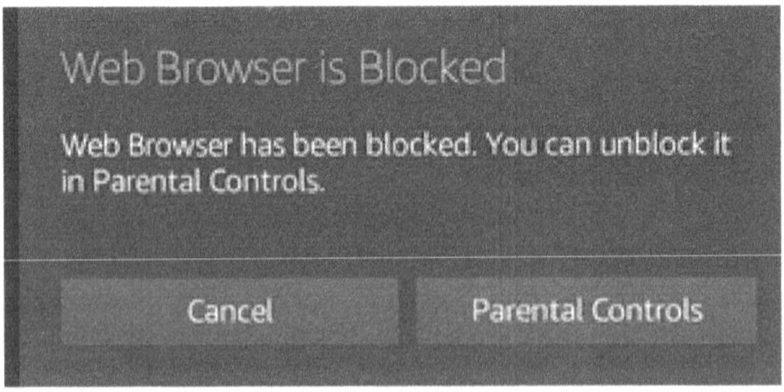

You can gain access only with your parental controls password. Enter the password, and your Fire will allow access to the content for the remainder of the current session. Once you put your Kindle to sleep or turn it off, when it is turned back on, parental controls will automatically password lock any use of the web browser.

The simple process described above will prevent your child from using the web browser in the Fire without knowing the password. You also want to take the time to make sure that all the content that is on the device itself is appropriate for your child's viewing. If there are any books, apps, videos, or games that your child shouldn't see, you can delete these from the device. Remember that a copy of everything you purchase from Amazon remains in your personal space in the Amazon cloud, and it can always be downloaded from the cloud at a later time if you need to view or use that content.

That's the short version of what you need to do to make your Fire safe for children. However, you have an array of flexible options that you can use to limit what your child can and cannot do with your Fire, if you're willing to take the time to set up these options. It's not that difficult a process, and the rest of this chapter will step you through this process.

About Kindle FreeTime

FreeTime, provided with every Fire HD6, can prevent unpleasant surprises on your credit card statement after you discover that your darling 6 year old daughter has been buying extra points for hours on end while playing her favorite video game over the past month. It will prevent your 10 year old twin sons from exploring the wonders of adult only web sites that they have no business visiting. And it can allow your children time to use their Fire, without letting the amount of time get completely out of control.

The Amazon Fire product line has become a phenomenally popular choice of tablet computer for the younger set, for a number of reasons. Older children such as teenagers may be better off with the more productivity oriented types of computers, such as a Windows or an Apple iOS-based laptop computer or a Microsoft Surface tablet. But younger children are generally interested in entertainment and education rather than productivity. In addition, the Fire is an economical choice: many parents understandably have qualms about spending the better part of a thousand dollars on a desktop or laptop computer with decent power for a child who falls in the under 10-years-of-age range.

Two features built into all models of the Fire HD6 make the tablet an ideal choice for children: **FreeTime**, and **FreeTime Unlimited**. FreeTime is an Amazon app that is a standard part of the Fire operating system. With FreeTime, parents can create individual password protected profiles for each of their children. Using the individual accounts, parents can select the books, apps, and videos that a particular child should be allowed to see, even when multiple children are sharing the same Fire. Once a child's profile has been set up under FreeTime, a special desktop appears on the Fire's screen whenever that child logs in to the device, and their desktop contains only the content the parent has selected for the child. The following illustration shows an example of the modified desktop that appears when the FreeTime app is activated.

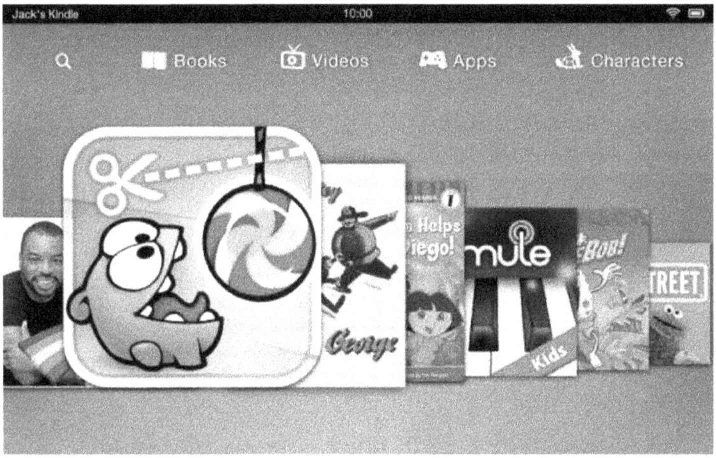

Besides providing excellent content management for children, the FreeTime app provided by Amazon also lets parents set time limits that govern the use of the device under each account. It may take some time up front to setup the multiple profiles needed when you have more than one child sharing a device in your household, but it is certainly worth the peace of mind in knowing that your children won't be watching inappropriate material, and won't be playing games on the Fire all evening when they are supposed to be devoting sometime to their school work. Much of this section of the chapter will provide you with the step-by-step directions you need to set up Kindle FreeTime on any family member's Fire HD6.

About FreeTime Unlimited

The other major addition that makes the Fire the choice for children is the availability of FreeTime Unlimited, a subscription service provided by Amazon and aimed specifically at children. FreeTime Unlimited provides a massive number of books, movies, and apps aimed specifically at children from ages 3 to 8, with prices at the time of this writing starting at $2.99 monthly per child and maxing out at $6.99 per month for up to 6 children (if you have an Amazon Prime membership). If you don't have on Amazon Prime membership, you're looking at a slightly higher monthly cost for 6 children.

On the videos side, much of what FreeTime Unlimited offers is older television titles such as Mister Rogers, Sesame Street, Bob the Builder, Kipper, and Mighty Morphin Power Rangers. On the apps side, FreeTime Unlimited gives you a wide assortment of learning apps for educational tasks such as learning to read, math skills, and playing musical instruments. And given Amazon's heritage in books, you would expect FreeTime Unlimited to deliver in the book area, and it does. Thousands of lavishly-illustrated children's titles are included in the FreeTime Unlimited subscription. Many of the titles that are provided for the young end of the spectrum- those just learning to read- include a feature called immersion reading. With this feature, the written text of the eBook is synchronized with an audio voice track, and young children see the words highlighted as the book is read to them.

In a nutshell, this sums up why you, as a parent, should choose the Fire HD6 as your child's tablet, and why you need to read this section of the book. You care about your child or children and you want to be sure that they use their Fire HD6 appropriately. At the same time, your life is hectic enough with the demands of parenthood, and you want to put a safe device into your child's eager hands with a minimal amount of hassle. You can make use of either of two powerful features of the

Fire HD6-- ***Parental Controls*** and ***Kindle FreeTime***-- that can be used to provide a safe and appropriate environment for your children.

Parental Controls, or Kindle FreeTime?

With two different methods of protecting and managing a child's use of a Fire, Parental Controls, and Kindle FreeTime, parents may be a bit confused as to which option is preferable. (At the Parental Controls setup screen, Amazon recommends Parental Controls for children aged 9 and older, and FreeTime for children of ages 8 and under; however, this is an admittedly subjective point, and different parents will have different ideas on this topic.) In a nutshell, here is what each option can do to keep your kids in a safe computing and media environment:

Parental Controls set overall limits on what anyone who uses your Fire can do without the Parental Controls password. It prevents children from making unauthorized purchases, from surfing the web, and (if desired) from playing videos, music, apps, or games. These types of content can be blocked on an individual basis, hence you might allow your children to read books and listen to music while choosing to block apps and videos. You cannot, however, set any time limits governing the amount of time that your children are allowed to use the Fire if you are solely using parental controls.

Kindle FreeTime, by comparison, goes farther in establishing precise controls on what children can and cannot do with your Fire HD6. With FreeTime, you can literally select the apps, videos, and reading materials that you've decided are appropriate for a child. You can also set time limits that control the amount of time your children can spend using the

Fire each day. You can do this for up to 6 different children on the same Fire HD6.

Setting up Kindle FreeTime is somewhat more complex than turning on Parental Controls. Hence, here is a general rule of thumb: If each child has their own individual Fire (HD6 or HD6 line), and daily time limits are not important to you, then Parental Controls are likely to suffice. In all other cases, you will likely want to opt for using Kindle FreeTime.

Activating Parental Controls

When Parental Controls are sufficient for providing a safe environment for a child, you can implement these controls with these steps, which were detailed at the start of this article. They are repeated here because this portion of the article explains each of the individual settings for Parental Controls.

Tap and drag down the status bar at the top of the screen, then tap the Settings icon at the far right to bring up settings for the Fire. Tap Parental Controls and change the setting from Off to On, and you will be asked to enter and reenter a password. Once you enter a password, parental controls will be enabled with the default settings, as shown in the illustration here.

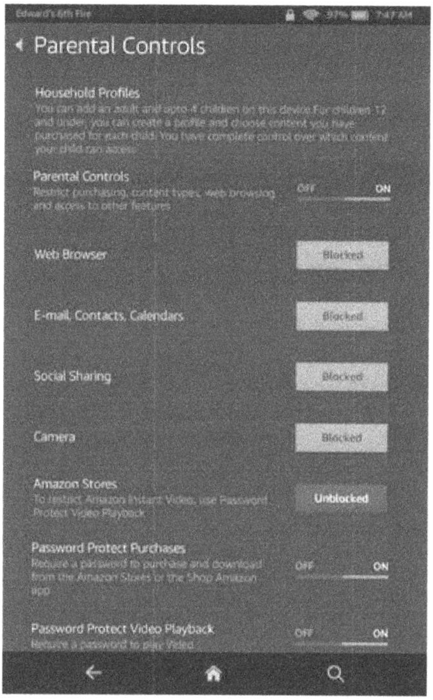

The first screen of the Parental Controls provides options for web browser, email contacts and calendars, password protected purchases, and access to a second screen that lets you block or unblock specific content types. Choosing the Block option for the web browser prevents the use of the browser unless the parental controls password is entered, and the block option for E-mail, Contacts, and Calendars prevents the use of all of these features unless the Parental Controls password is entered.

The Password Protect Purchases option is also set to On by default. With this option turned on, the Parental Controls password must be entered before any purchases can be made through the Amazon store. Just below this option is the Password Protect Video Playback option. If this option is turned on, videos cannot be played on the Fire without the use of the Parental Controls password.

The 'Block and unblock content types' option, when tapped, leads to another screen with you lets you block or unblock specific content types, as shown in this illustration.

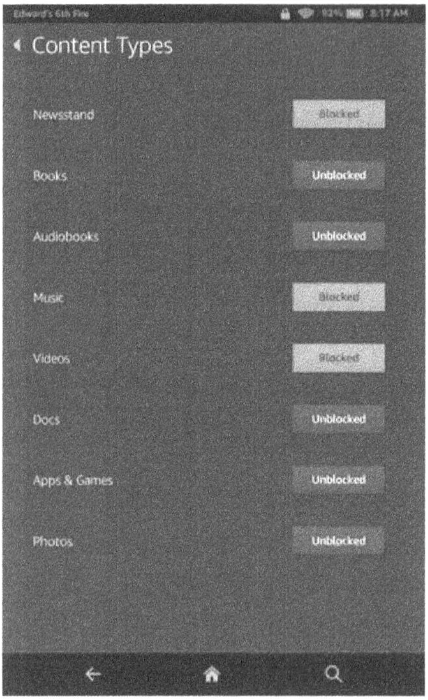

As shown in the illustration, you can choose to individually block newsstand content, books and audiobooks content, music, video, documents, apps and games, or photos, by individually pressing the button at the far right for each content type.

Finally, if you return to the first Parental Controls Settings screen and scroll upwards, you see three additional options at the bottom of the screen: Change Password,

Password Protect Wi-Fi, and Password Protect LBS (Location-Based Services). The Change Password option lets you change the parental controls password (you will be asked to enter both the old and the new passwords). Turn on the Password Protect Wi-Fi option, and your children will be required to enter a password to access Wi-Fi for any reason. Turning on the Password Protect Location-Based services option will then require a password to be entered before any location based services (GPS) can be accessed by any apps or other software that is installed on the Fire.

Kindle FreeTime

When you want more precise control over your children's tablet habits then Parental Controls offers, such as when you have multiple children of various ages using the same Fire HD6, or you want to control the amount of time your children are allowed to use the tablet each day, Kindle FreeTime is your obvious choice. When you use FreeTime, you as the parent can select the apps, videos, and games that you want each child to be able to see, and you can set time limits for videos, for apps, or for reading books separately, as well as setting a total screen time. You can create separate profiles for up to 6 children on any single Fire HD6. Note that FreeTime also-

- blocks web browser access
- blocks any purchases in the Amazon store
- disables social networks Facebook and Twitter
- requires password entry for purchases or to turn wireless connectivity on

Installing FreeTime

FreeTime can be found in the Apps Library of your Fire HD6. Tap Apps, then tap Cloud, and look for the Kindle FreeTime app icon, as shown here.

Tap the icon to download and install FreeTime. When the installation process is completed, you will see an opening screen welcoming you to FreeTime, as shown in the following illustration.

When the opening screen appears, tap the Get Started button at the lower right corner of this screen. A screen requesting a lock screen password next appears, as shown in the following illustration:

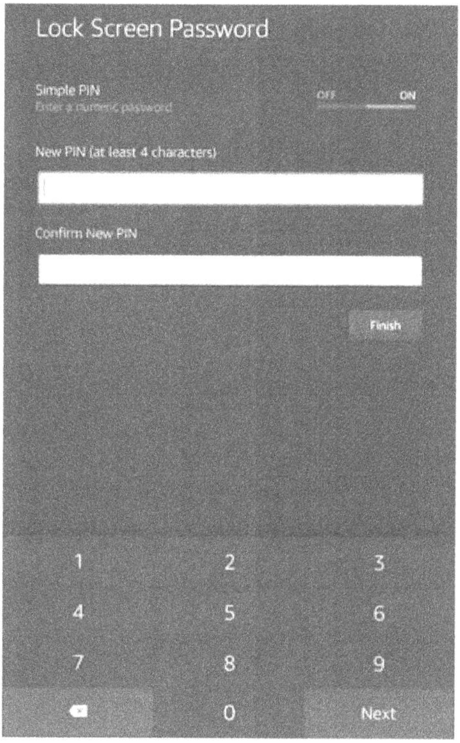

Your first step in setting up FreeTime is to create a lock screen password that keeps children from exiting their profiles without your permission. Enter a numeric PIN of four or more numbers, and confirm it by entering it a second time when prompted, then click Next.

The next step in the setup process for FreeTime involves creating a profile for each of your children that will use this Fire. Perform the following steps to create a profile:

1. Select the 'Tap to set Photo' option to select a profile photo (each child using the Fire HD6 can have a different photo assigned to help them to remember their profile).

2. Enter your child's name, birthdate, and gender in the Add Child Profile screen that appears, then tap Next.

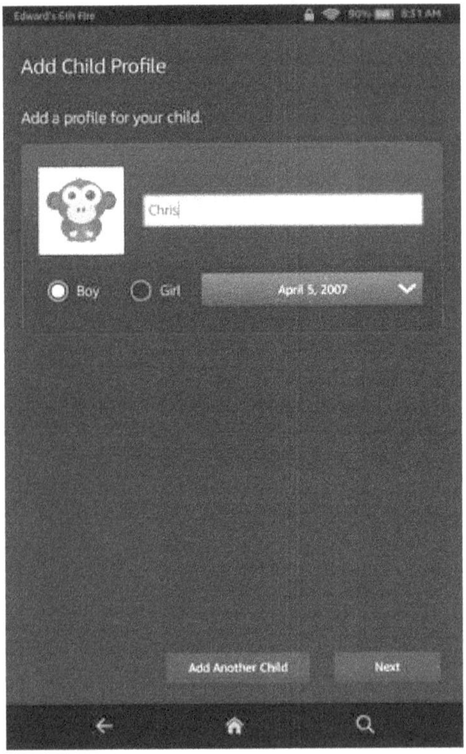

As many as six different profiles can be created on any Fire HD6. After you create each child's profile, you can tap 'Add Another Child' at the bottom of the screen if you need a profile for an additional child. When done entering profiles for all your children, tap 'Next' at the bottom of the screen.

After you tap 'Next,' you will see an advertisement for FreeTime Unlimited, a subscription service provided by

Amazon and aimed specifically at children (detailed earlier in this chapter under the heading 'About FreeTime Unlimited').

If you wish to enroll in FreeTime Unlimited, tap the desired option (single-child or family plan); if not, tap the 'No thanks' button to proceed.

Once you've created profiles for the children in your household, you will need to add the desired content to each of the profiles. You can add books, TV shows, movies and apps you already own to a child's profile, using the following steps:

1. Once inside the Kindle FreeTime app, tap Manage Content at the bottom of the screen, and enter your Parental Controls password when asked. A 'Manage Content &

Subscription' screen will appear, as shown in the following illustration.

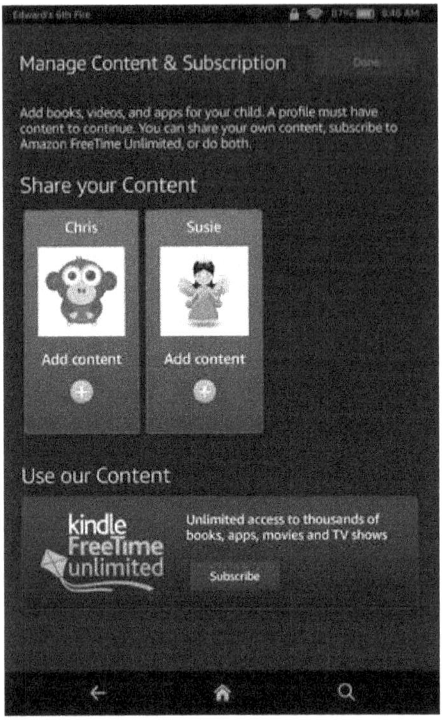

2. Tap the Add Content tab representing the desired child's name.

3. Turn on the checkboxes beside the books, videos or apps that you want to add to the child's library. (The following illustration shows an example.)

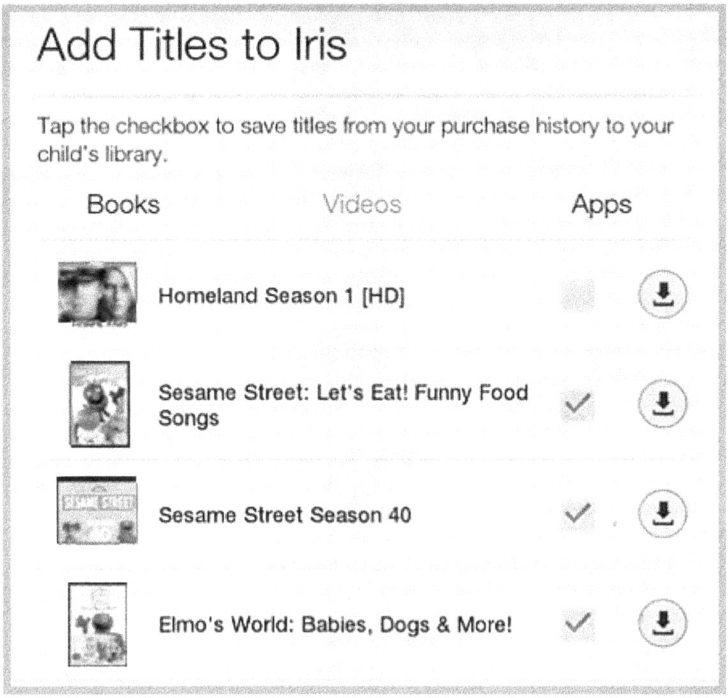

5. Tap Save.

6. For your changes to be permanent, you must exit the FreeTime App. To do this, pull the Status Bar down from the top of the screen and tap Exit FreeTime, or, if you are in the Settings screen, tap the Exit icon. To exit, you must enter the Parental Controls password.

Using the Fire with FreeTime

Once FreeTime has been set up for the children in your household, a login icon appears at the upper left. Tap that icon, and icons for all household users of the Fire appear, as shown in the following illustration:

When a child taps the icon for his or her profile, the desktop that appears on the Fire shows only those books, videos, and apps that you have given permission for your child to use. (If you tap the icon representing your profile, you must enter the lock screen password to gain access to your Fire.)

NOTE *You can also manage the content that is available in your child's FreeTime Library while you are logged into your Amazon account through a web browser. To manage your child's content from your browser, go to* ***http://www.amazon.com/manageyourkindle****. At the screen that appears, look for the link at the left that reads* ***Kindle Free Time Settings*** *and click this link. The next screen that you see (shown in the example that follows) can be used to set up and manage*

FreeTime settings for each of up to six children per Fire.

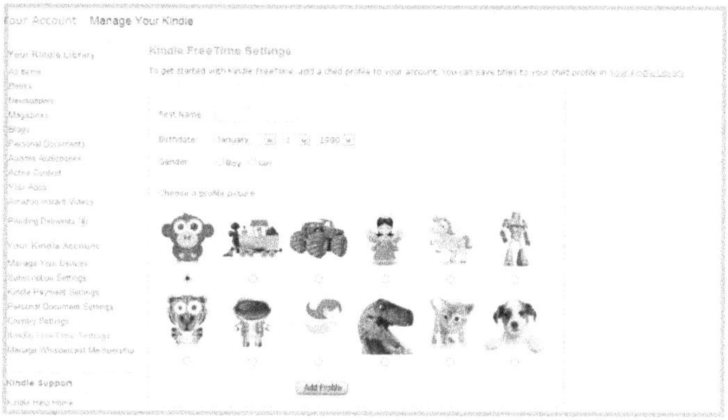

Setting Time Limits on Your Child's Profiles

Another major feature of the FreeTime app for the Fire HD6 is that you can set time limits for the amount of time that each child is allowed to use the device. You can set these time limits on an individual basis; for example, you could limit your 8-year old to one hour of apps use daily, while providing three hours of reading time daily, while your 12-year old gets two hours of daily apps use and unlimited reading time. Or you might allow unlimited access to books, while blocking all access to videos.

Note that on the Fire HD6, games are included in the FreeTime apps library. Therefore, whatever time limits you apply to a child's use of apps will also apply to that child's use of games. Use the following steps to set up time limits:

1. From any FreeTime screen, swipe down the Status Bar at the top of the screen, and tap Settings.

2. You will be prompted for your Parental Controls password. Enter the password, and tap OK.

3. Tap Set Daily Time Limits, then tap the profile you want to update.

4. Besides the Set Time Limits option, tap On.

5. Limit your child's activity by total screen time or specify specific time limits by content activity.

6. Under Total Screen Time, move the slider as desired to specify the maximum time that your child can spend using any content under FreeTime.

7. Under Content Activity Time, move the slider as desired to control the time that your child is allowed to watch videos, use apps/games, or read books. (Moving the slider to the far right allows for unlimited time, while setting the slider at the far left will block all access to that type of content.)

8. Pull the Status Bar down from the top of the screen and tap Exit FreeTime. Enter your Parental Controls password when prompted, and the changes will take effect.

At this point, your Fire HD6 is ready for use by the children of your household. One point that you'll want to keep in mind is that as your children grow older and as you purchase new content, you'll likely want to update their profiles accordingly.

Chapter 12: Printing from your Fire HD6

The Fire HD6 is one of a new generation of Amazon Fire products that support wireless printing, allowing you to print from your Fire HD6 directly to a variety of printers. Assuming that your printer supports wireless printing, you can print emails, contact details, calendar events, photos, personal documents, and web pages from the Silk browser from your Fire Tablet.

You cannot print personal documents that have been converted to Kindle format (.azw) through the Kindle Personal Documents Service.

Before you can print from your Fire HD6, you must first download a print plugin from the Amazon Appstore onto your Fire HD6. A list of compatible printers can be found on the product detail page for each of the plugins. The websites for these plugins are listed below; point your Silk browser at the link that corresponds to your model of wireless printer.

Epson: www.amazon.com/dp/B00ENB2CSK

HP: www.amazon.com/dp/B00EDUTGB2

Canon: www.amazon.com/dp/B00E19FB28

Samsung:

www.amazon.com/dp/B00DMZ3AM0

Ricoh: www.amazon.com/dp/B00FAX29AG

After downloading the plugin, make sure your printer is turned on and connected to Wi-Fi. You can then press and hold the item you'd like to print, and then tap Print in the popup menu that appears. Choose your printer from the list of printers that appears, tap OK, and then tap Connect. If your printer isn't listed, tap to search for additional printers, or tap to add a printer manually using the IP address of the printer. If you don't know your printer's IP address, refer to your product's user guide for assistance.

Finally, choose the number of copies you want to print, or tap More options to choose the Color Mode, Paper Size, or Orientation. Tap Print to begin printing.

What if my printer is not on the above list?

Support for wireless printing is a relatively new printer feature at the time of this writing. As a result, the above process cannot be used with many existing printers. Fortunately, all is not lost in these cases—you may not have to shell out the costs of a new printer just to be able to print on your Fire HD6. With the right combination of apps and free services, you can print directly from your Fire. You can use Google Cloud Print, a free service that is linked to a Google account, to print to Wi-Fi printers that are compatible with Google Cloud Print. Once you set up Google Cloud Print to work with a wi-fi printer, you'll need an app like EasyPrint. (You can click the link shown to get to the EasyPrint download page on the Amazon website.)

First, get a Google account if you don't already have one, and set up Google Cloud Print using your Google account. You can find full instructions explaining how to do